# EASY PIANO
# POPULAR SHEET MUSIC
## 30 HITS FROM 2015-2017

ISBN 978-1-4950-9330-2

HAL•LEONARD®

7777 W. BLUEMOUND RD. P.O. BOX 13819 MILWAUKEE, WI 53213

Visit Hal Leonard Online at
**www.halleonard.com**

# ADVENTURE OF A LIFETIME

Words and Music by GUY BERRYMAN,
JON BUCKLAND, CHRIS MARTIN,
WILL CHAMPION, MIKKEL ERIKSEN
and TOR HERMANSEN

**Moderately fast**

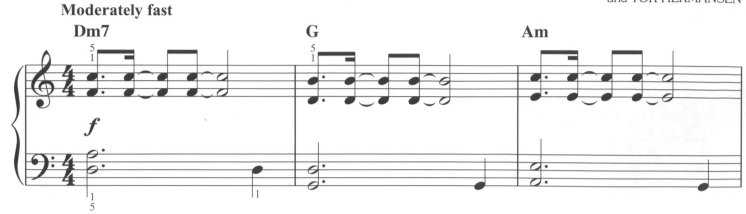

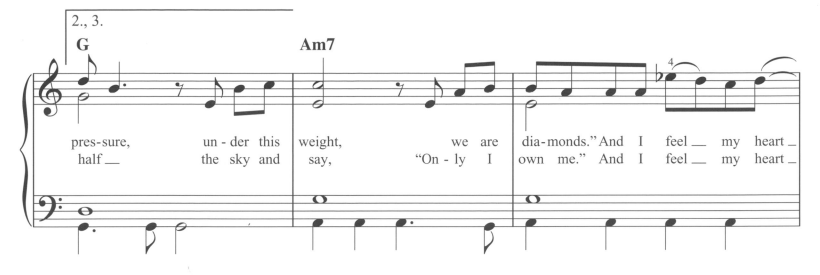

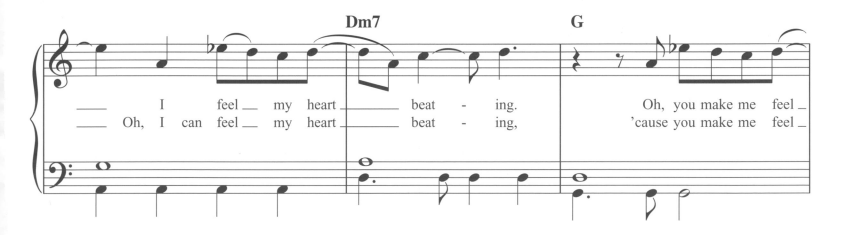

(A - live   a - gain.)

Oh,  you make me    feel ____

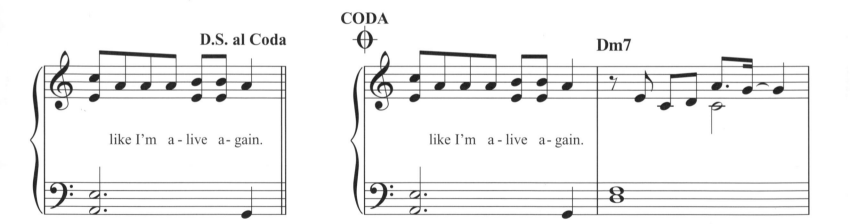

like I'm  a - live  a - gain.

like I'm  a - live  a- gain.

"Turn your mag-ic

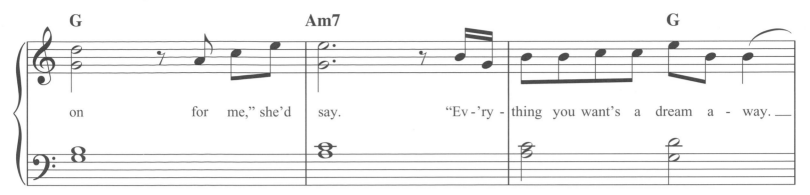

on       for   me," she'd   say.      "Ev-'ry-|thing you want's a dream a - way.

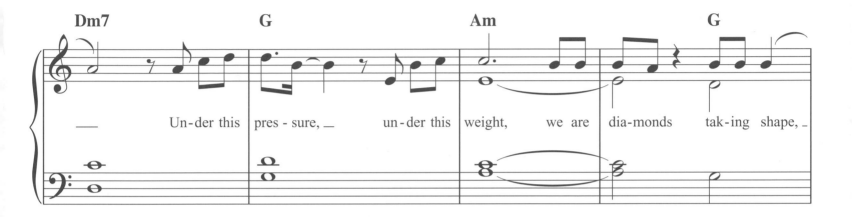

Un-der this | pres - sure,   un-der this | weight,    we are | dia-monds tak-ing shape,

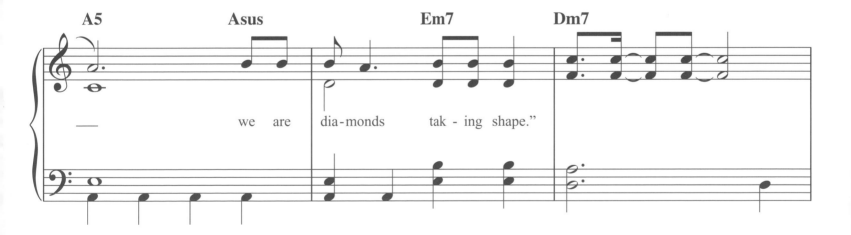

we   are | dia-monds   tak - ing shape."

6

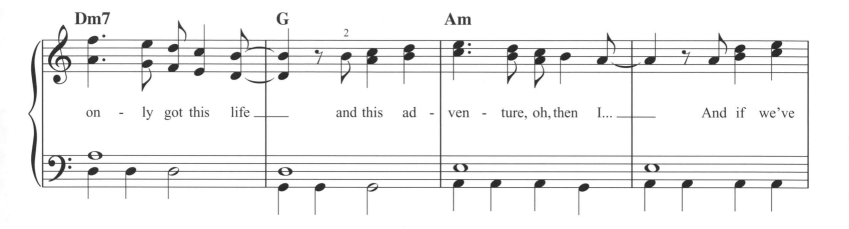

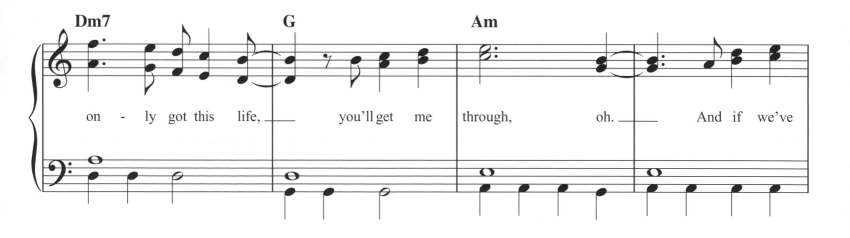

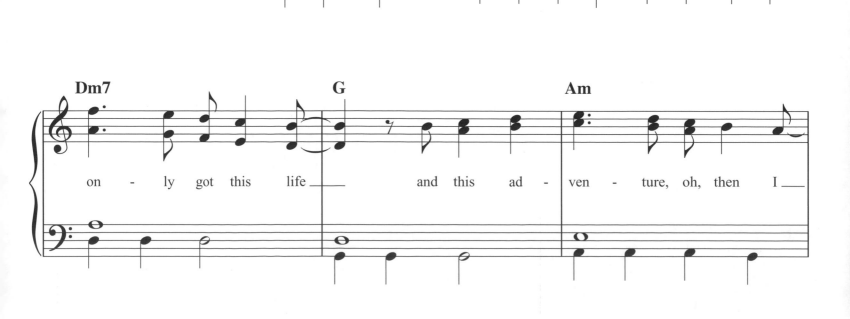

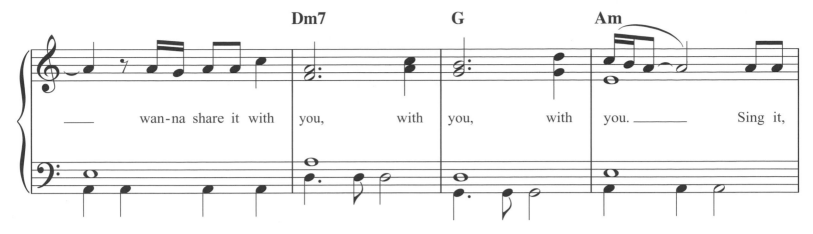

# BURN
## from HAMILTON

Words and Music by
LIN-MANUEL MIRANDA

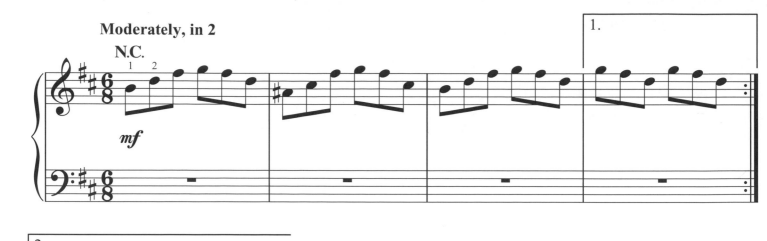

I saved ev-'ry let-ter you wrote me. ____

From the mo-ment I read them I knew you were mine. You said you were

mine. I thought you were ____ mine. ____ Do you know what An-

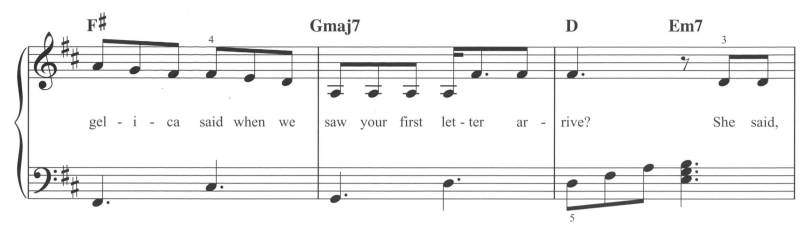

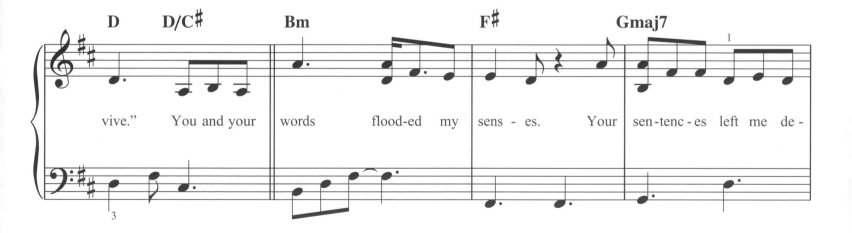

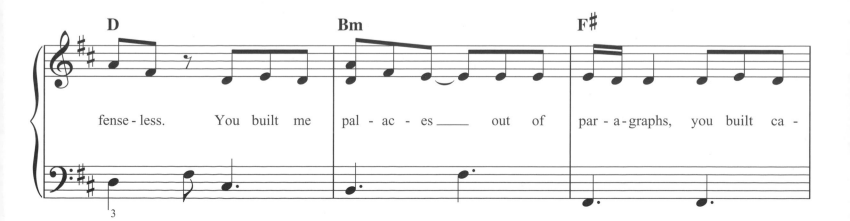

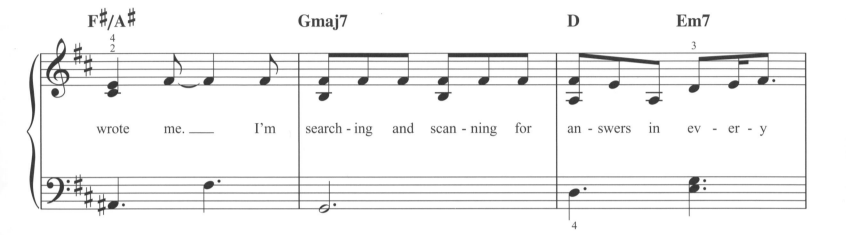

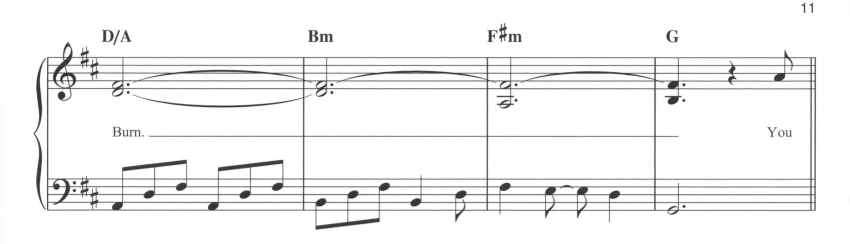

Burn. _____ You

pub - lished the let - ters she wrote you. ___ You told the whole world how you

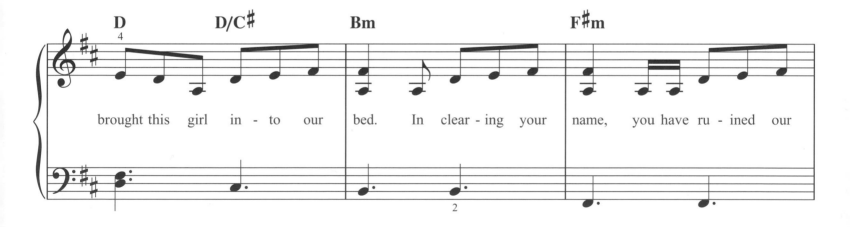

brought this girl in - to our bed. In clear - ing your name, you have ru - ined our

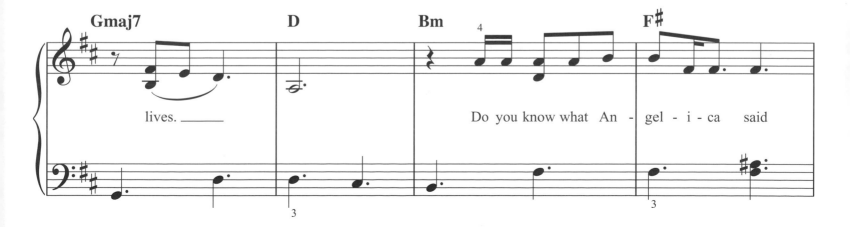

lives. _____ Do you know what An - gel - i - ca said

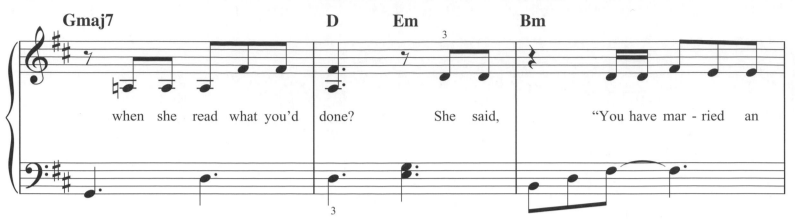

when she read what you'd done? She said, "You have mar - ried an

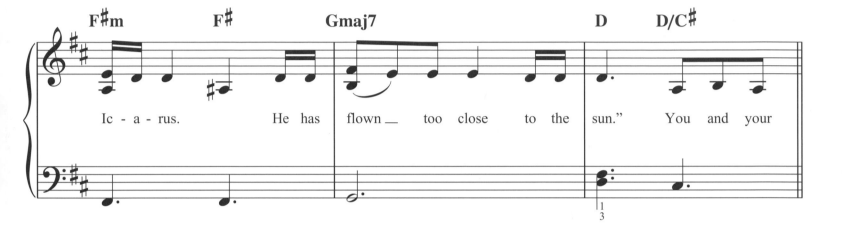

Ic - a - rus. He has flown ___ too close to the sun." You and your

words, ob - sessed with your leg - a - cy... Your sen - tenc - es bor - der on

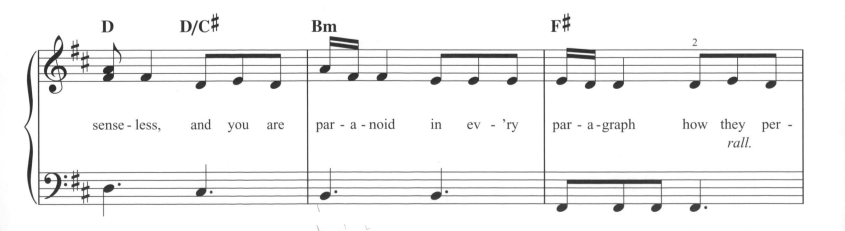

sense - less, and you are par - a - noid in ev - 'ry par - a - graph how they per -
*rall.*

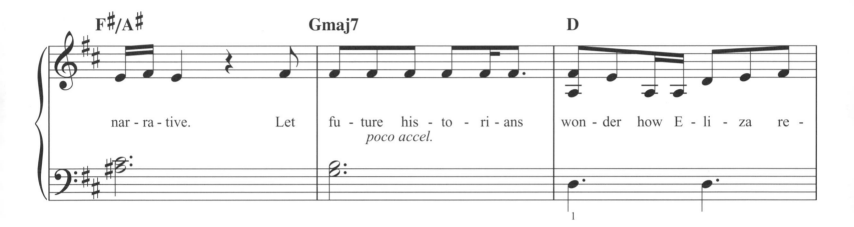

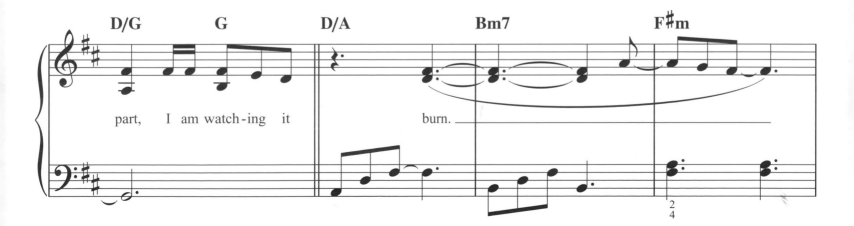

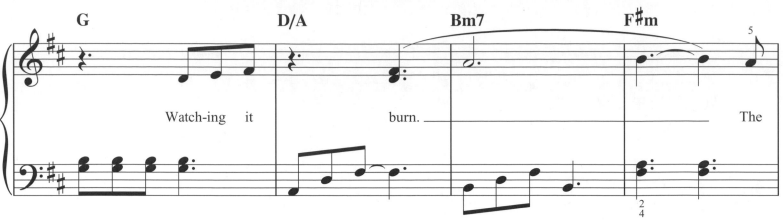

Watch-ing it burn. _____ The

world has no right to my heart. The world has no place in our bed. They

don't get to know what I said. I'm burn - ing the mem - o - ries, burn - ing the

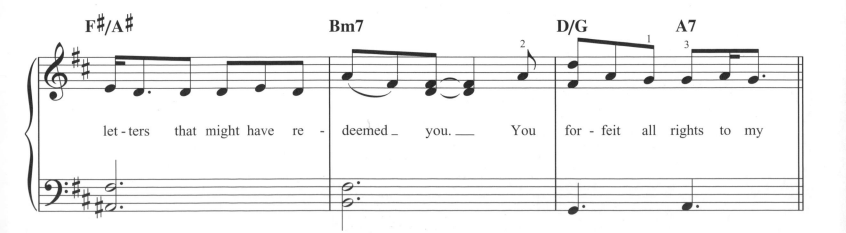

let - ters that might have re - deemed _ you. _ You for - feit all rights to my

heart. You for-feit the place in our bed. You sleep in your of-fice in-

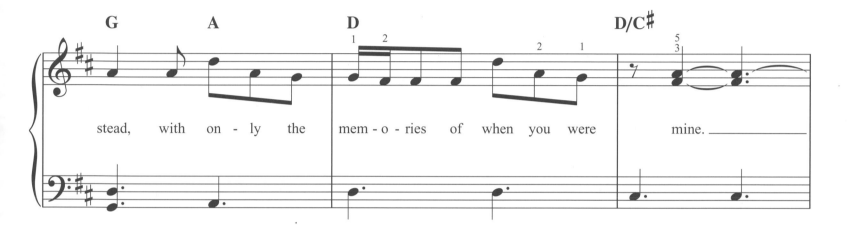

stead, with on-ly the mem-o-ries of when you were mine.

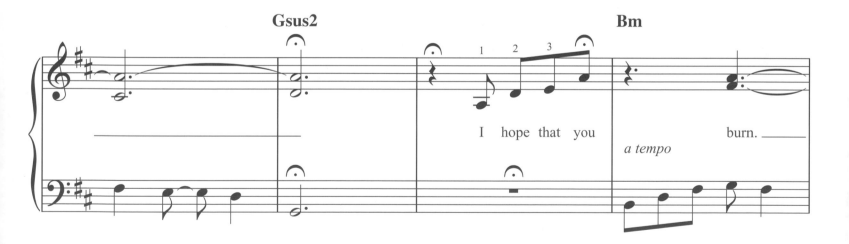

I hope that you burn.
*a tempo*

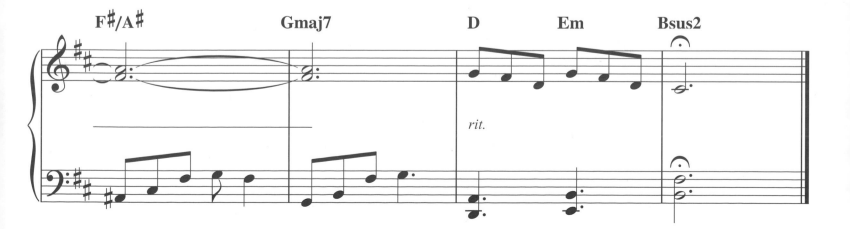

*rit.*

# CARRY ON

Words and Music by
NORAH JONES

And af - ter all's been said and done, who said it best?
the time to done speak and speak to me,

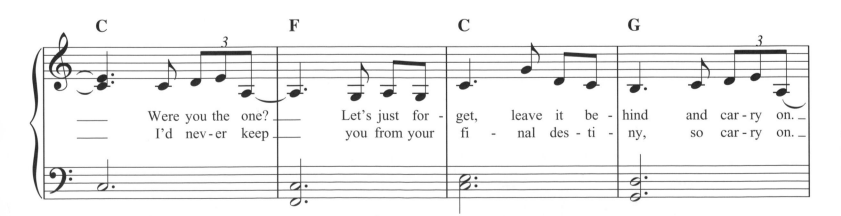

Were you the one? Let's just for - get, leave it be - hind and car - ry on.
I'd nev - er keep you from your fi - nal des - ti - ny, so car - ry on.

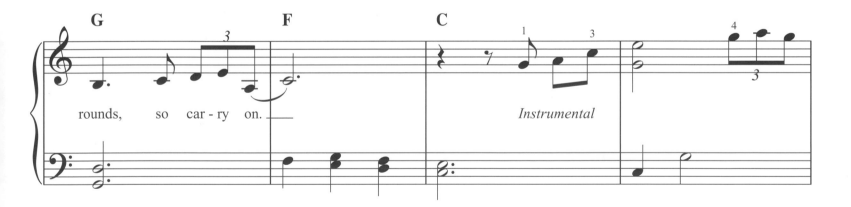

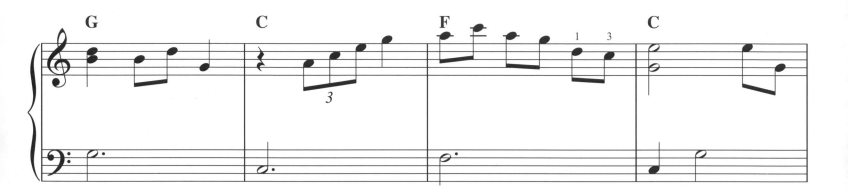

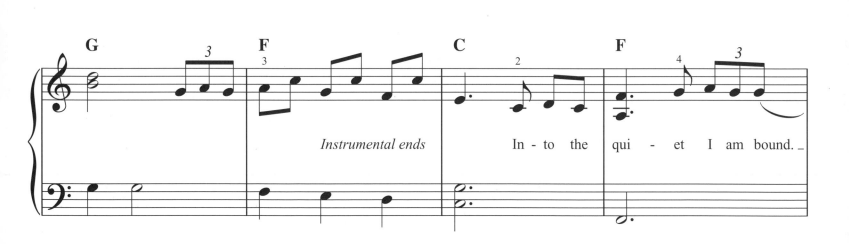

*Instrumental ends*

In - to the qui - et I am bound. __

__ What you have lost, __ I've nev - er found. __ I lost my nerve, yet peace sur -

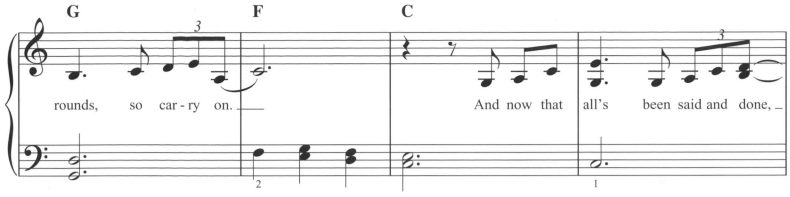

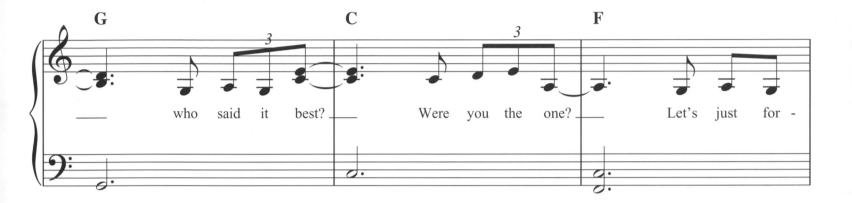

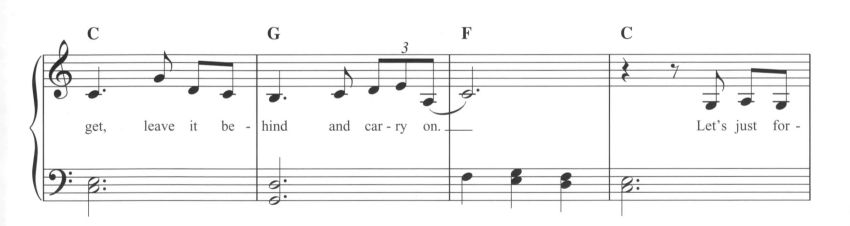

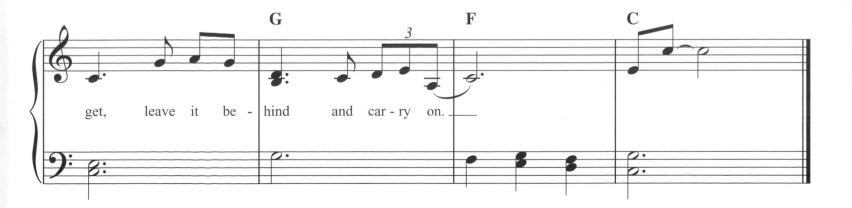

# CHEAP THRILLS

Words and Music by SIA FURLER,
GREG KURSTIN and SEAN PAUL HENRIQUES

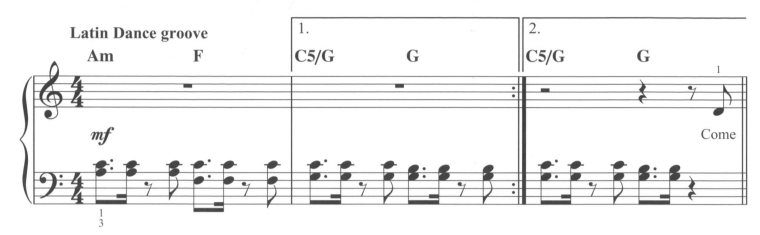

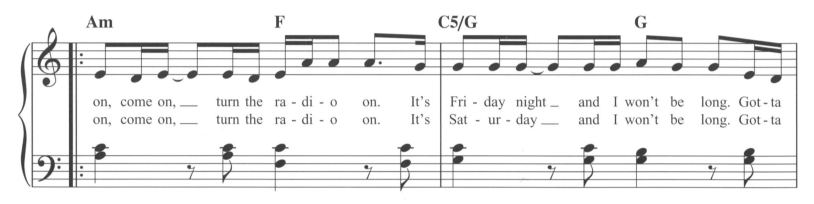

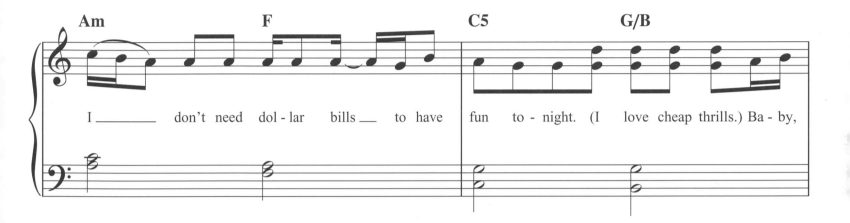

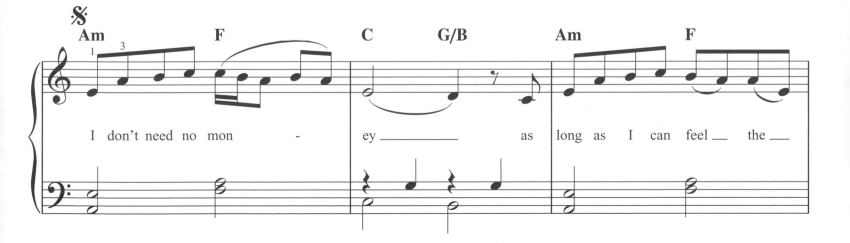

beat. _____ I don't need no mon - ey _____ as

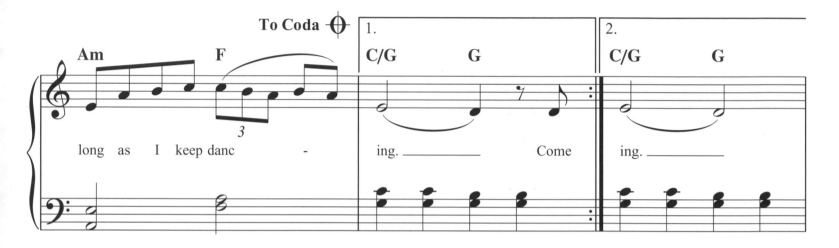

long as I keep danc - ing. _____ Come ing. _____

I don't need no mon -

ey _____ as long as I can feel __ the __ beat. _____

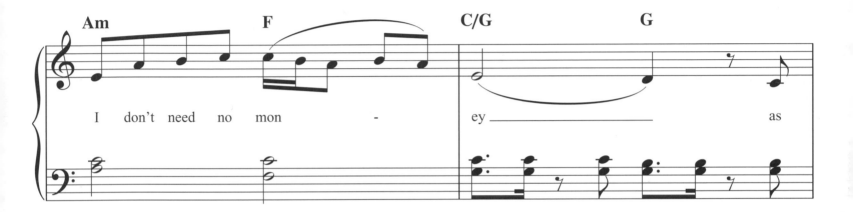

I don't need no mon - ey _____ as

long as I keep danc - ing. (Oh, oh, oh.) Ba - by,

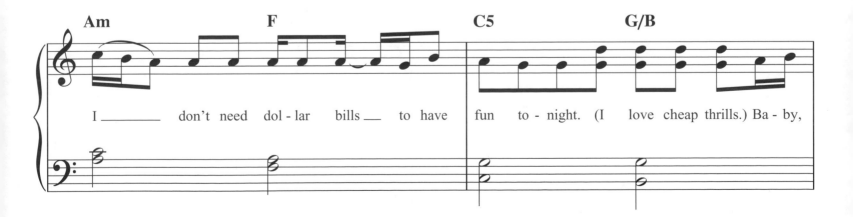

I _____ don't need dol - lar bills __ to have fun to - night. (I love cheap thrills.) Ba - by,

# CITY OF STARS
## from LA LA LAND

Music by JUSTIN HURWITZ
Lyrics by BENJ PASEK & JUSTIN PAUL

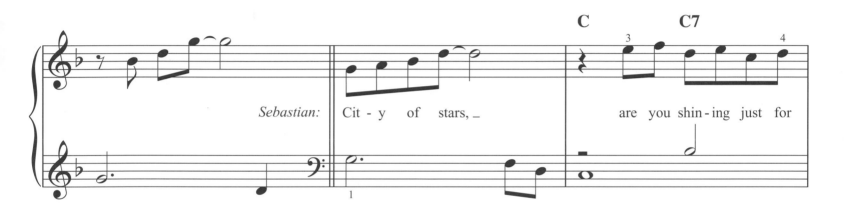

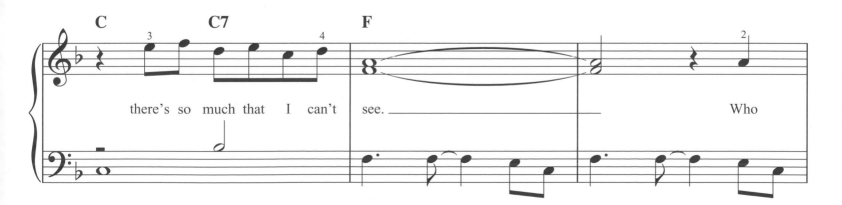

knows?                I felt it from the first em - brace    I shared with

you        *Mia:* that    now        our        dreams    may    fi - n'lly    come

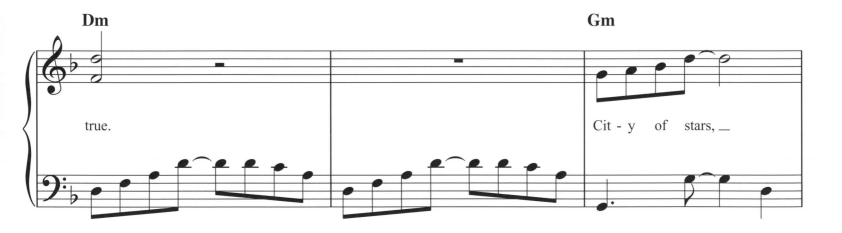

true.                                              Cit - y    of    stars, __

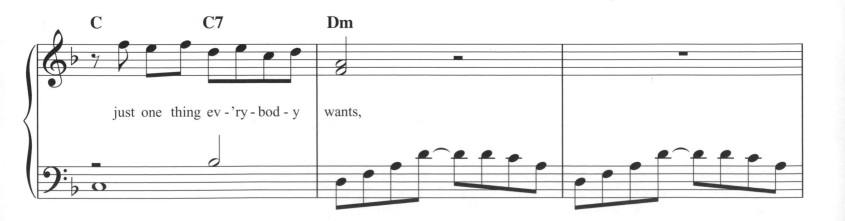

just one thing ev -'ry - bod - y    wants,

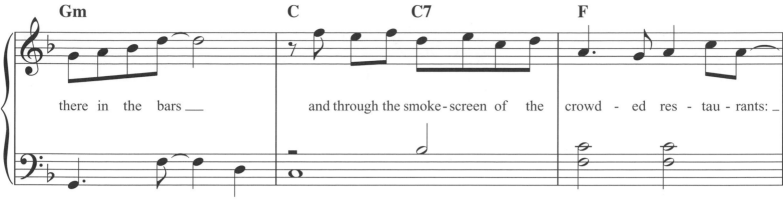

there in the bars ___ and through the smoke-screen of the crowd-ed res-tau-rants: ___

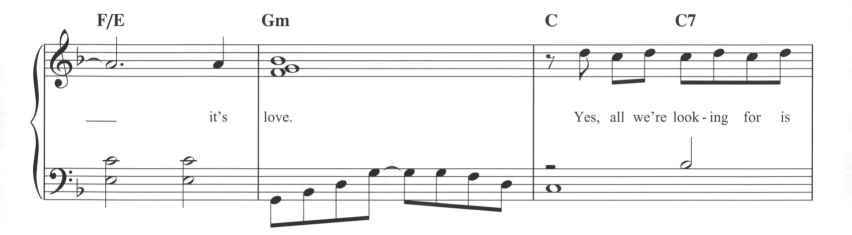

___ it's love. Yes, all we're look-ing for is

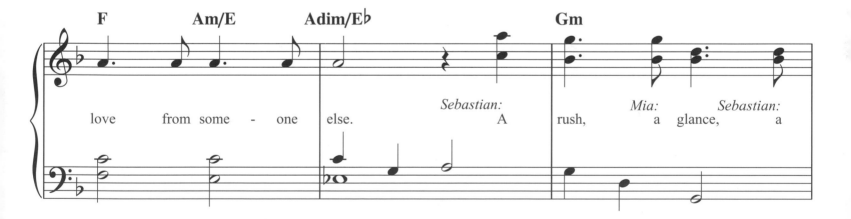

love from some-one else. *Sebastian:* A rush, *Mia:* a glance, *Sebastian:* a

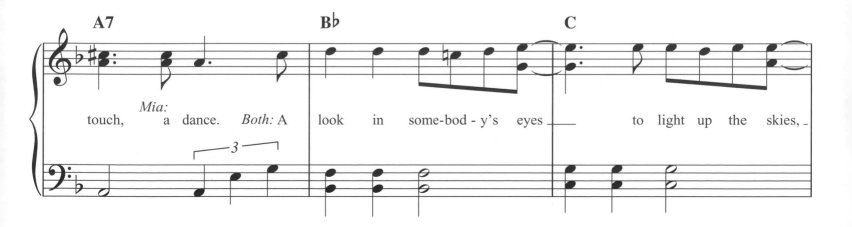

*Mia:* touch, a dance. *Both:* A look in some-bod-y's eyes ___ to light up the skies, ___

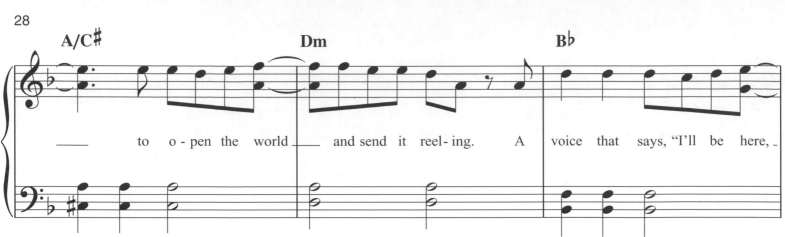

to o-pen the world ____ and send it reel-ing. A voice that says, "I'll be here,

____ and you'll be al - right." ____

I don't care if I know ____ just where I will go, ____ 'cause all that I need's

____ this cra-zy feel-ing, a rat - tat - tat on my heart...

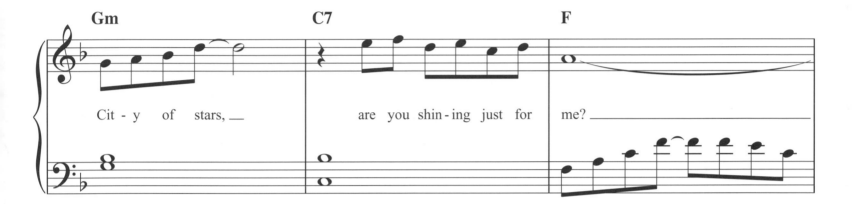

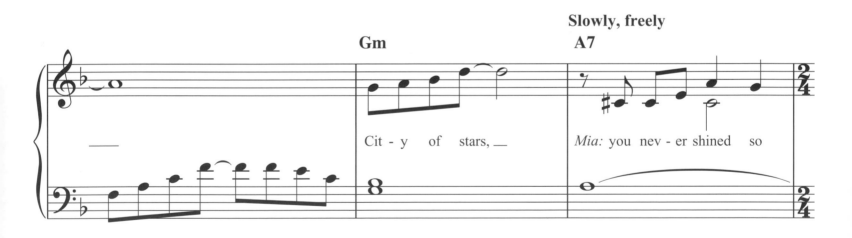

# DON'T WANNA KNOW

Words and Music by ADAM LEVINE,
BENJAMIN LEVIN, JOHN HENRY RYAN,
AMMAR MALIK, JACOB KASHER HINDLIN,
ALEX BEN-ABDALLAH, KENDRICK LAMAR,
KURTIS McKENZIE and JON MILLS

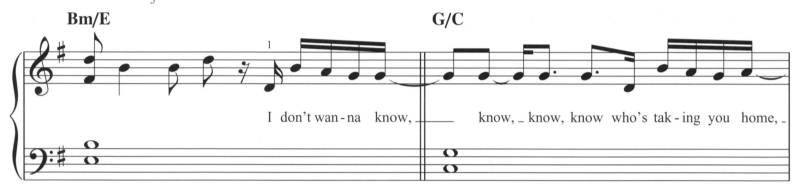

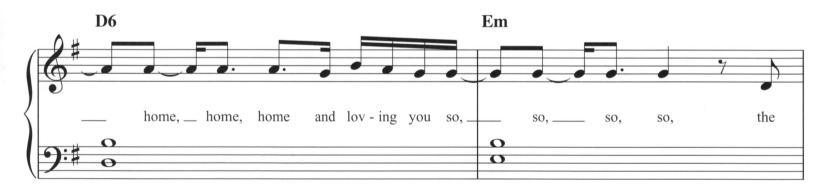

think of \_\_\_ me, \_\_\_ of what we used to \_\_\_ be? \_\_\_ Is it bet - ter \_\_\_ now \_\_\_ that I'm

not a - round? \_ My friends all act - ing \_\_\_ strange; \_ they don't bring up your \_\_ name. \_\_ Are you

hap - py \_\_\_ now? \_\_\_ Are you hap - py \_\_\_ now? \_\_\_ I don't wan - na know, \_

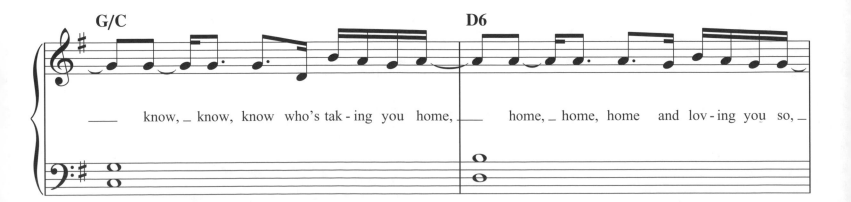

\_\_\_ know, \_ know, know who's tak - ing you home, \_\_\_ home, \_ home, home and lov - ing you so, \_

so, so, so, the way I used to love you. No, I don't wan-na know,

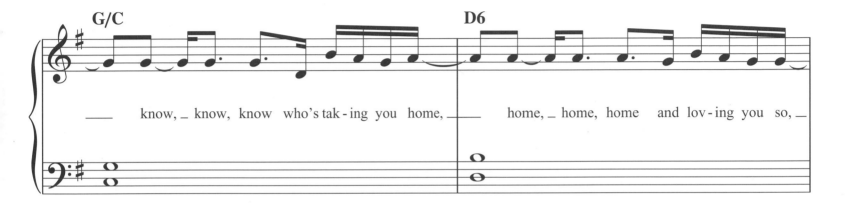

know, know, know who's tak-ing you home, home, home, home and lov-ing you so,

**To Coda** ⊕

so, so, so, the way I used to love you. Oh, I don't wan-na know.

And ev-'ry time I go out, yeah, I hear it from this

**Em7**

one, hear it from that __ one, that you got some - one new, __ yeah.

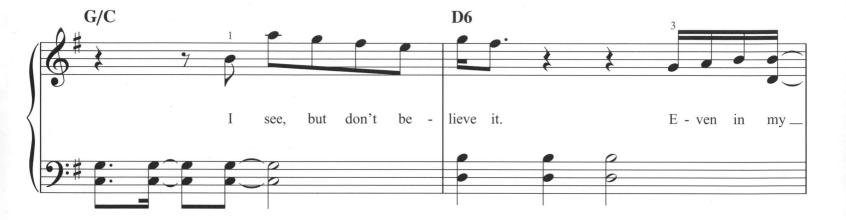

**G/C**  **D6**

I see, but don't be - lieve it. E - ven in my __

**Em7**  **D.S. al Coda**

__ head, you're still in my __ bed. May-be I'm just __ a fool. __ Do you

**CODA**

**G/C**  **D6**  **Em**

Wast - ed; and the more __ I drink, the more I think a-bout __ you.

And I know __ I can't take __ it.

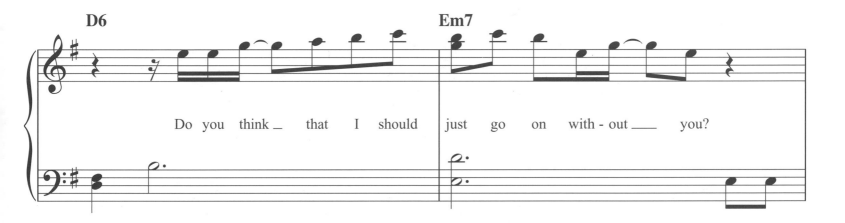

Do you think __ that I should just go on with-out __ you?

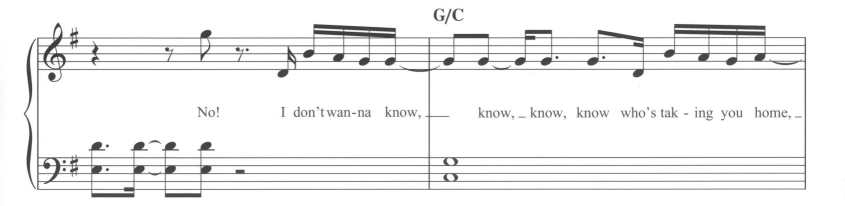

No! I don't wan-na know, __ know, __ know, know who's tak - ing you home, __

__ home, __ home, home and lov - ing you so, __ so, __ so, so, the

way I used __ to love you. No, I don't wan-na know, ____ know, know, know who's tak-ing you home, __

__ home, __ home, home and lov-ing you so, __ so, __ so, so, the

way I used __ to love you. Oh, I don't wan-na know.

# FRESH EYES

Words and Music by ANDY GRAMMER,
IAN KIRKPATRICK and ROSS GOLAN

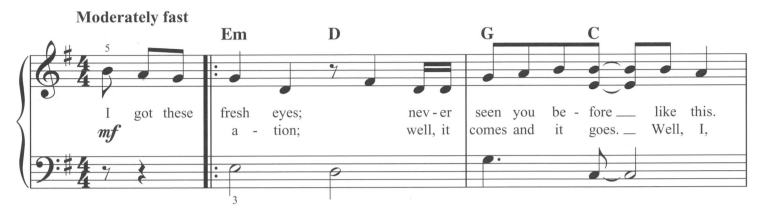

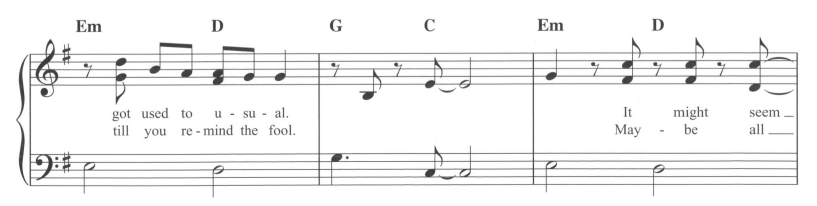

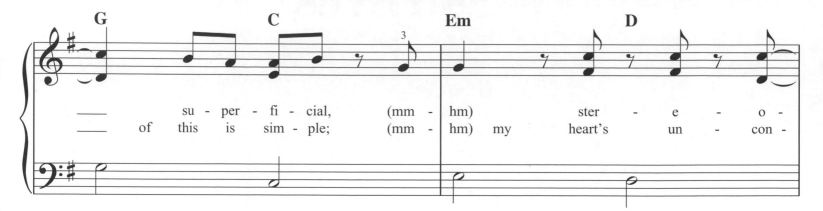

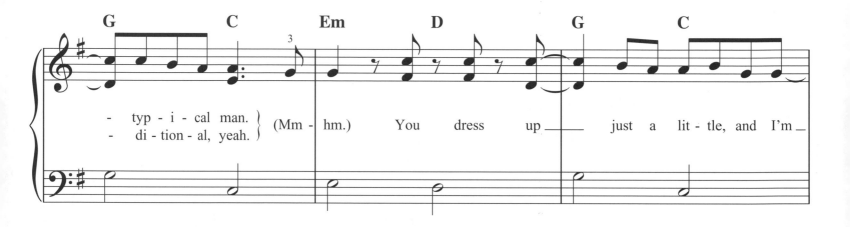

Now, all I see is you _____ with fresh eyes, fresh

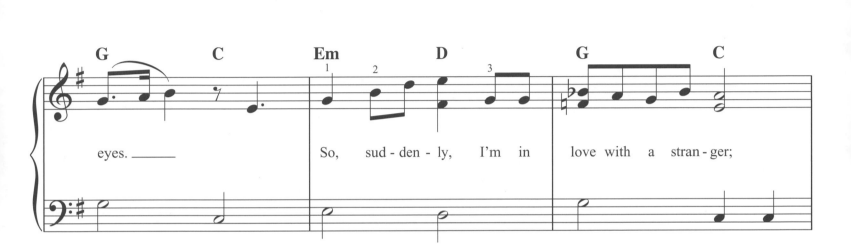

eyes. ____ So, sud-den-ly, I'm in love with a stran-ger;

I can't be-lieve that she's mine, _____ yeah. And now, all I see is you_

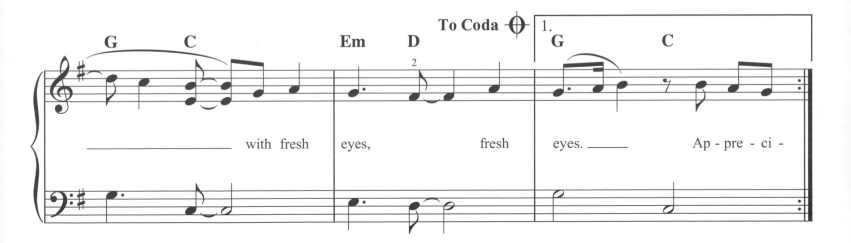

____ with fresh eyes, fresh eyes. ____ Ap-pre-ci-

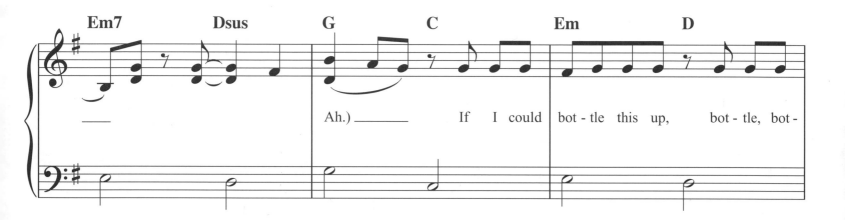

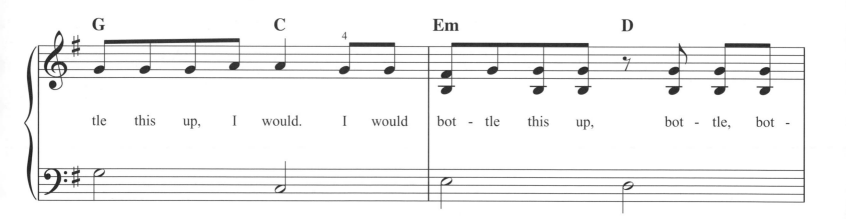

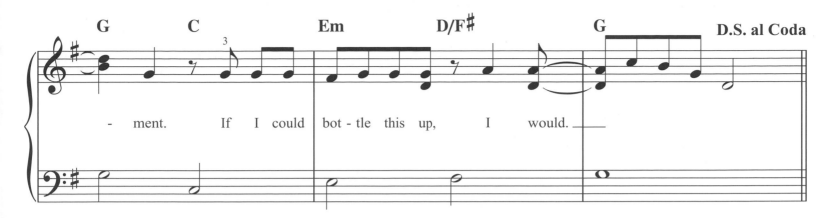
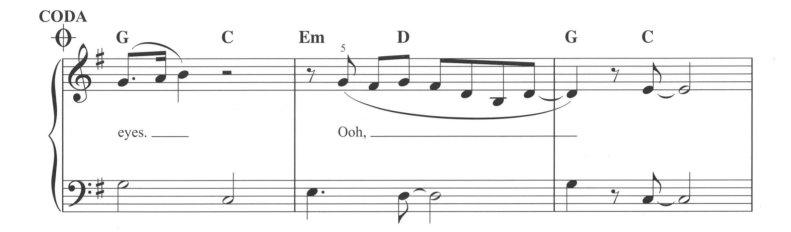
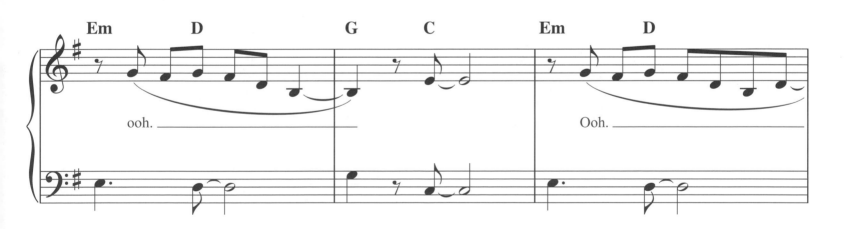
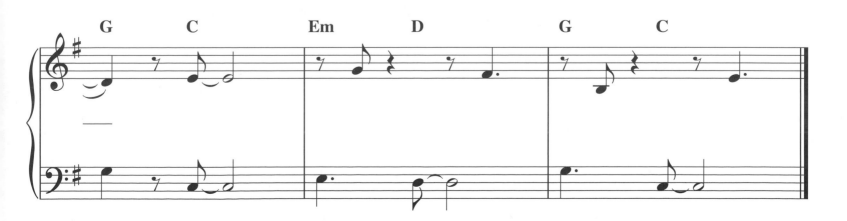

# HANDCLAP

Words and Music by ERIC FREDERIC,
SAMUEL HOLLANDER, MICHAEL FITZPATRICK,
JOSEPH KARNES, JAMES KING,
JEREMY RUZUMNA, NOELLE SCAGGS
and JOHN WICKS

**Dance beat**

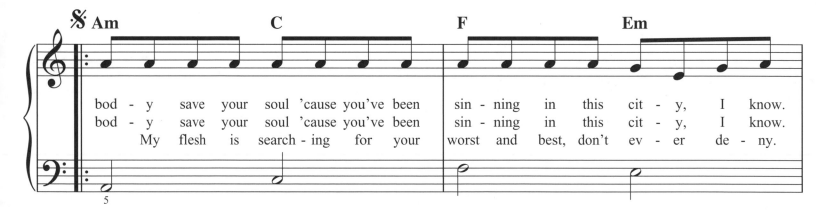

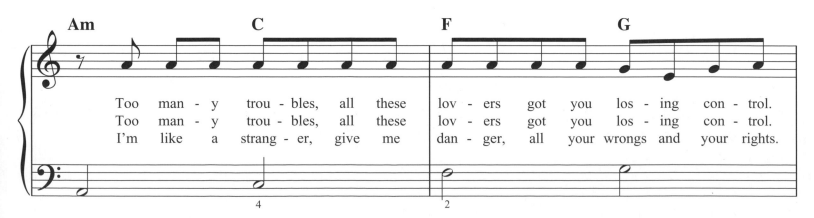

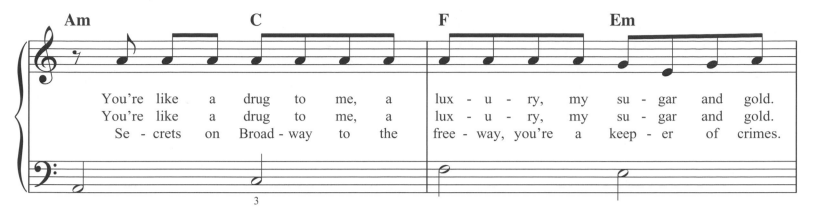

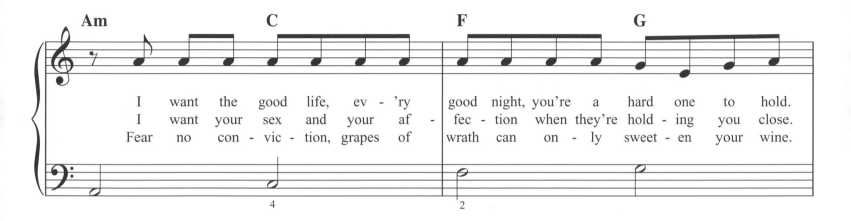

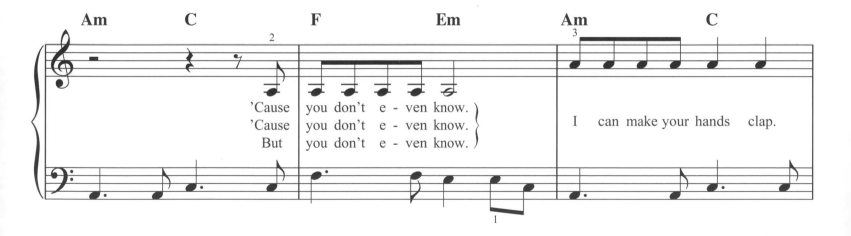

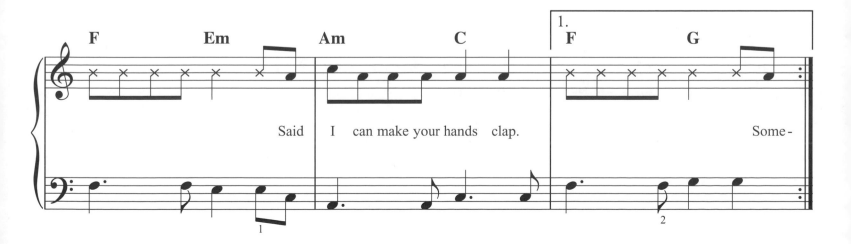

44

2., 3.

Ev - er - y night ____ when the stars come out, ____

____ am I the on - ly liv - ing soul a - round? ____ Need to be - lieve ____

____ you could hold me down ____ 'cause I'm in need ____ of some-thing good right

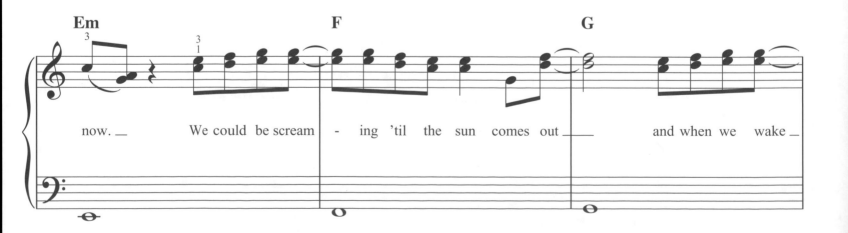

now. ____ We could be scream - ing 'til the sun comes out ____ and when we wake ____

_____ we'd be the on - ly sound. _____ Get on my knees _____ and say a prayer, James

Brown, _____ that I can make your hands clap.

**To Coda**

That

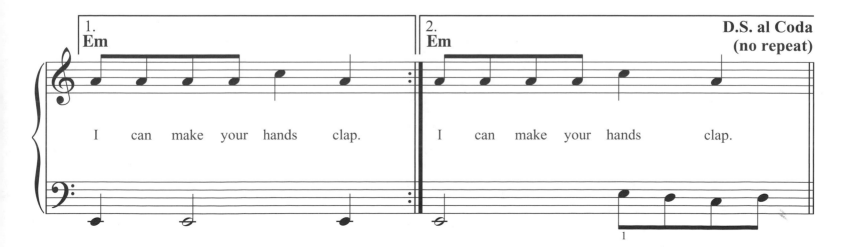

**1.**
I can make your hands clap.

**2.**
I can make your hands clap.

**D.S. al Coda**
**(no repeat)**

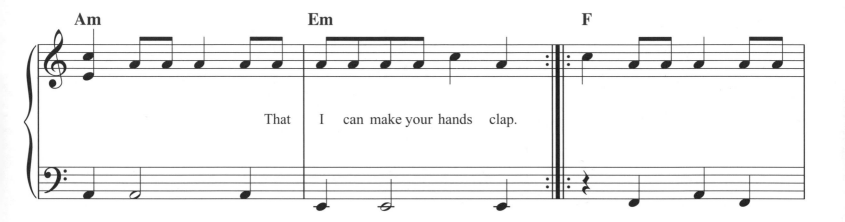

That     I    can make your hands    clap.

That     I    can make your hands      clap.
So     can   I   get   a     hand      clap?

1

# LET IT GO

Words and Music by JAMES BAY
and PAUL BARRY

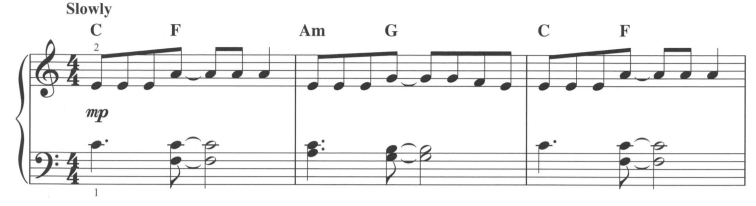

From walk - ing home and talk - ing loads,

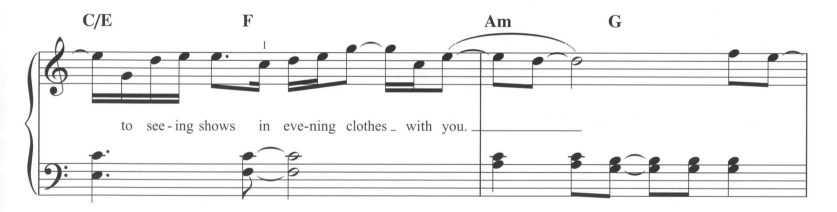

to - see - ing shows   in eve - ning clothes _ with you. _

From ner - vous touch   and get - ting drunk, _

to stay-ing up and wak-ing up ___ with you. ___ But now we're

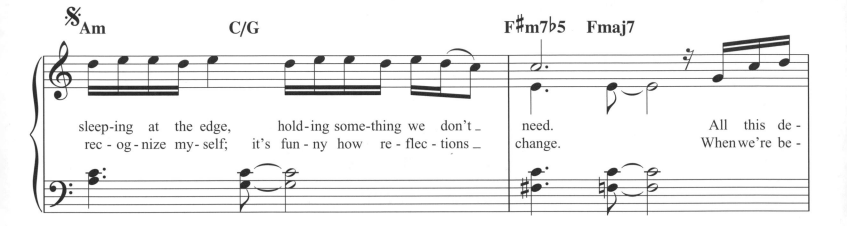

sleep-ing at the edge, hold-ing some-thing we don't _ need. All this de-
rec-og-nize my-self; it's fun-ny how re-flec-tions _ change. When we're be-

lu-sion in our heads is gon-na bring us to our ___ knees.}
com-ing some-thing else, I think it's time to walk a - way. }

So, come on, let it

go, ___ just let it be. ___ Why don't you be

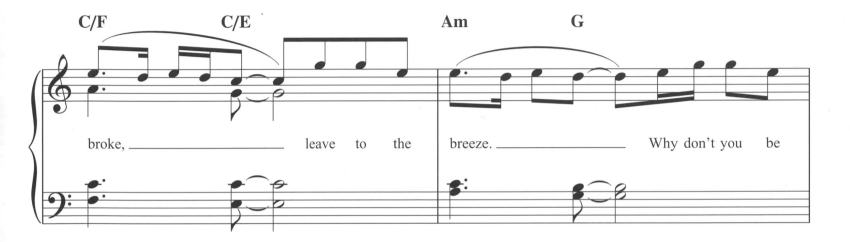

From throw-ing clothes a-cross the floor,

to teeth and claws, and slam-ming doors ___ at you. ___

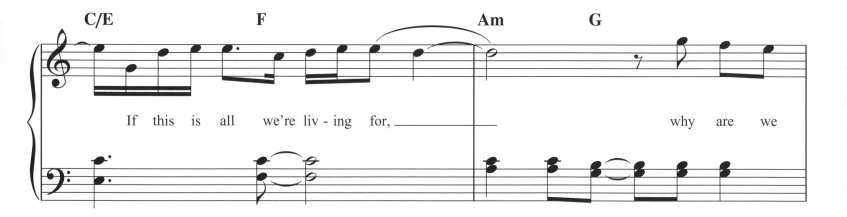

If this is all we're liv-ing for, ___ why are we

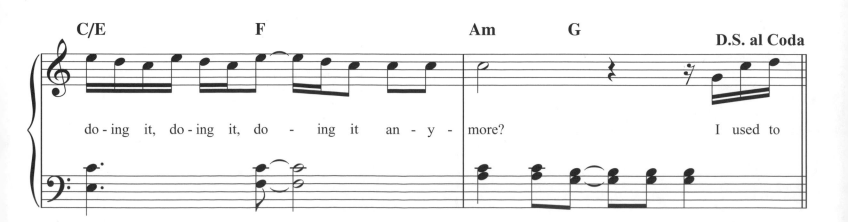

do-ing it, do-ing it, do - ing it an-y-more? I used to

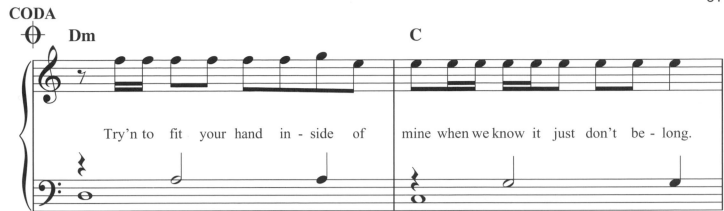

Try'n to fit your hand in - side of mine when we know it just don't be - long.

There's no force on earth could make __ it feel right, no. ____ Whoa. ____

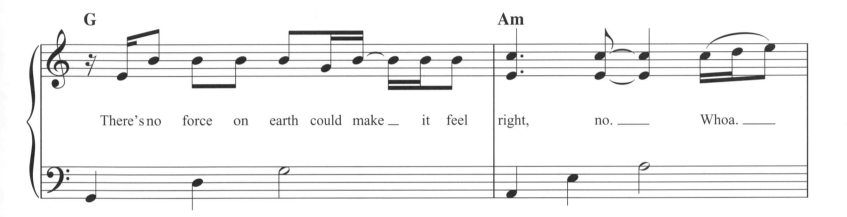

Try'n to push this prob - lem up the hill when it's just too heav - y to hold. __

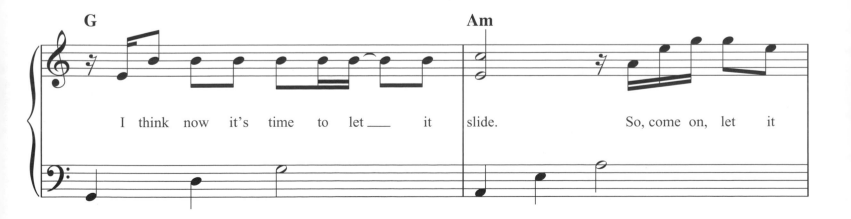

I think now it's time to let __ it slide. So, come on, let it

go,  oh, _____ just let it  be. _____ Why don't you be

you _____ and  I'll __ be  me?  Ev - 'ry - thing  that's

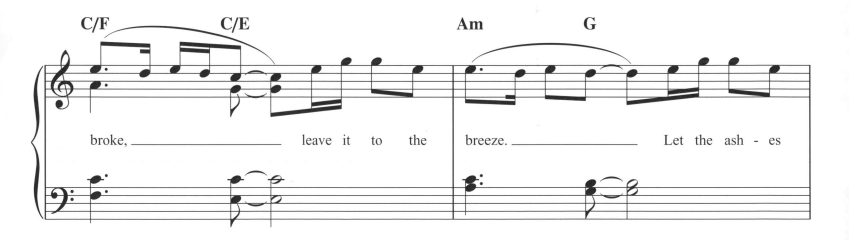

broke, _____ leave it to the  breeze. _____ Let the ash - es

fall; _____ for - get a - bout  me. _____ Come on, let it

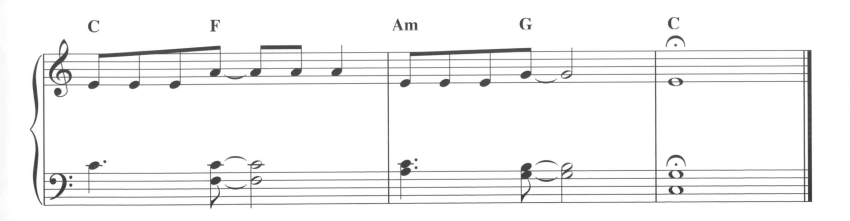

# HIDE AWAY

Words and Music by BRITTEN NEWBILL,
GINO BARLETTA, SCOTT BRUZENAK,
BRETT McLAUGHLIN and GRACE TANDON

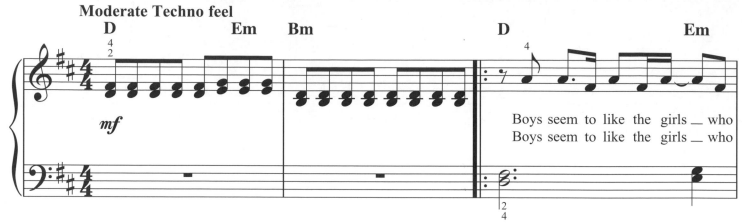

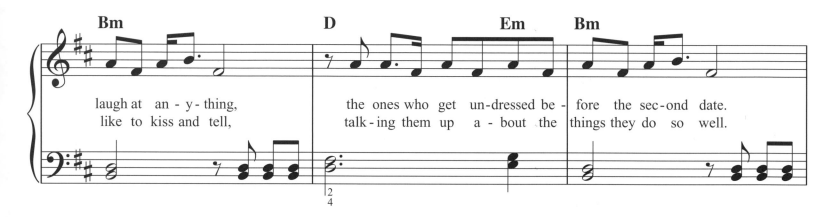

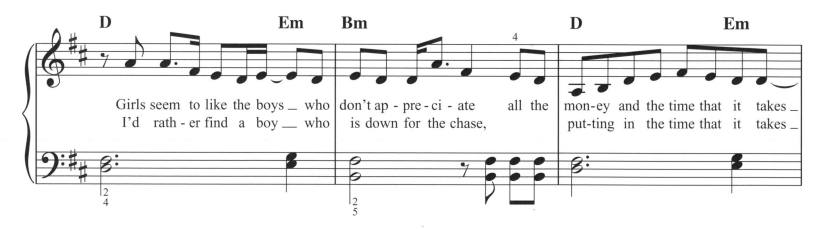

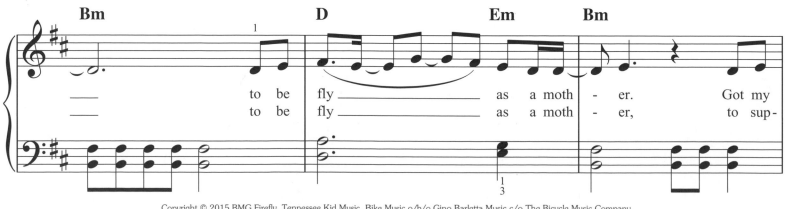

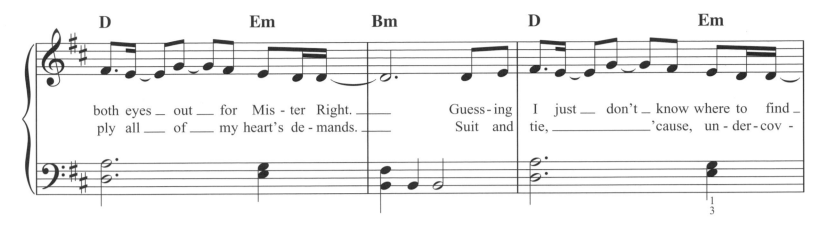

both eyes \_ out \_ for Mis - ter Right. \_\_\_
ply all \_ of \_ my heart's de - mands. \_\_\_

Guess - ing I just \_ don't \_ know where to find \_
Suit and tie, _____ 'cause, un - der - cov -

\_\_ 'em, but I hope they \_ all \_\_ come out to - night. \_
- er, he's gon - na save my \_ life \_ like Su - per - man. \_

Where do the good boys go to hide a - way, \_ hide a - way? I'm a

good, good girl who needs a lit - tle com - pa - ny. Look - ing high and low. Some - one

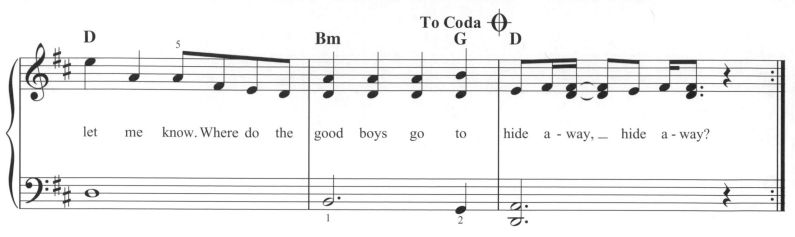

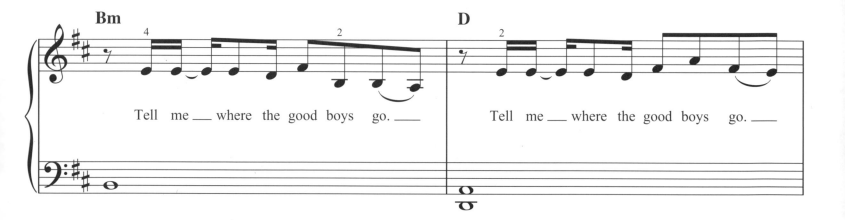

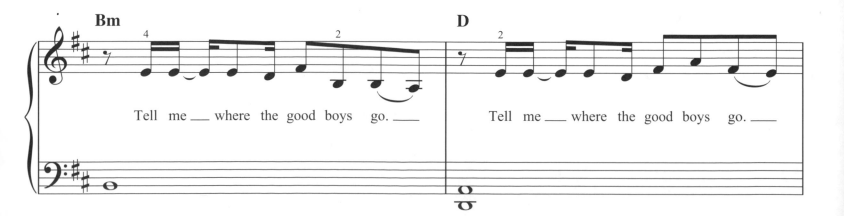

D.S. al Coda

**Bm**          **D**

Tell me __ where the good boys go. __ Tell me where the good boys go. Where do the

**CODA**

**D**       **Bm**    **G**    **D**

hide a - way, __ hide a - way?         Hide a - way, __ hide a - way.

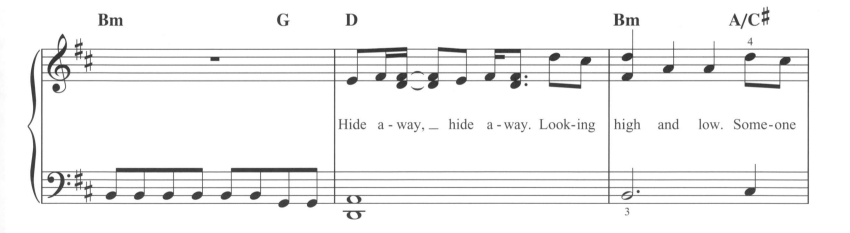

**Bm**     **G**   **D**           **Bm**    **A/C#**

Hide a - way, __ hide a - way. Look-ing high and low. Some-one

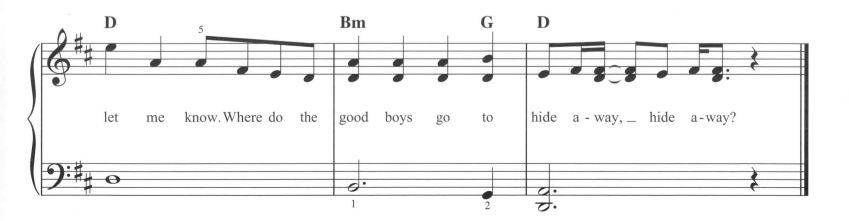

**D**            **Bm**    **G**   **D**

let me know. Where do the good boys go to hide a - way, __ hide a - way?

# H.O.L.Y.

Words and Music by busbee,
NATE CYPHERT and WILLIAM WIIK LARSEN

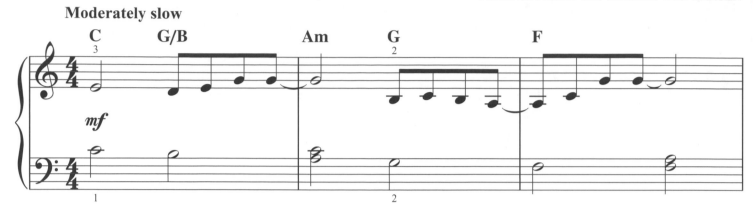

When the sun had left __ and the win-ter came __

and the sky - fall __ could on - ly bring the rain, __ I sat in dark - ness,

all bro-ken-heart - ed. I could-n't find a day __ I did-n't feel a - lone. __

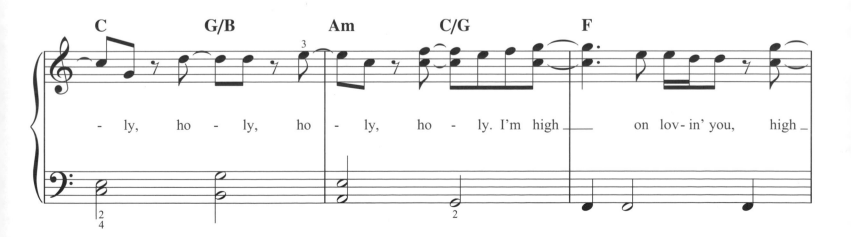

60

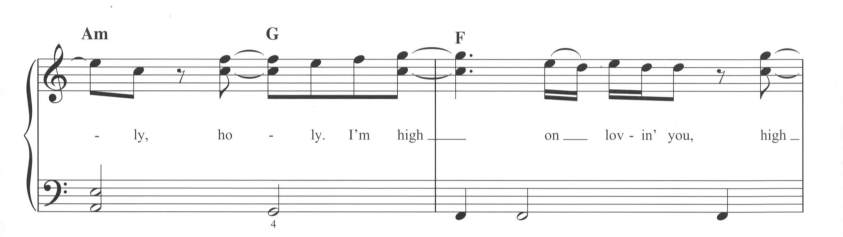

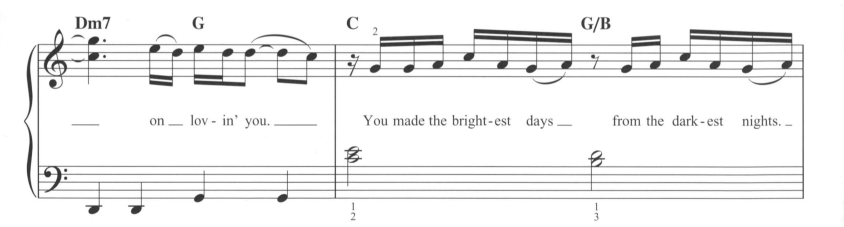

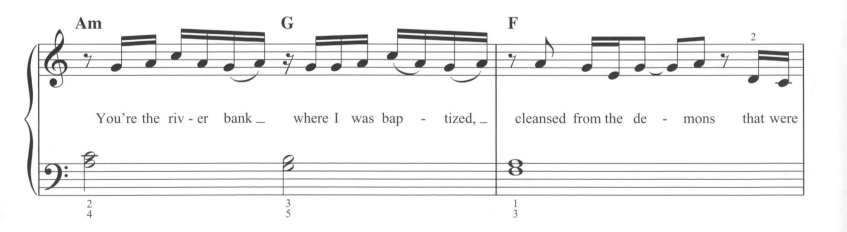

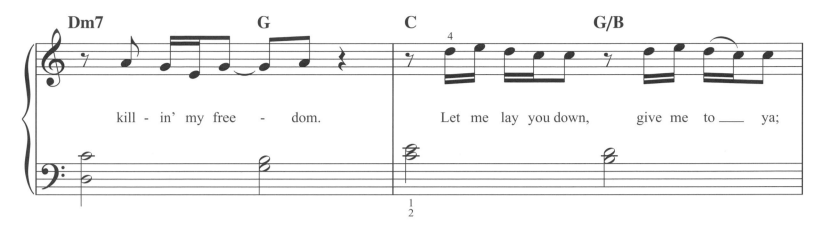

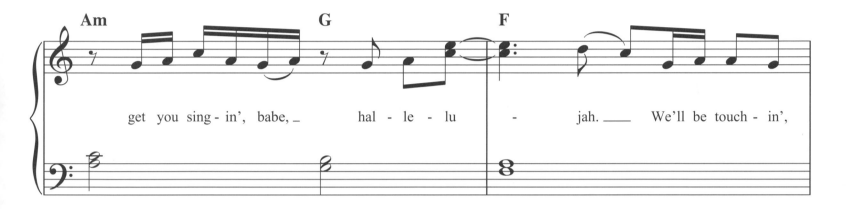

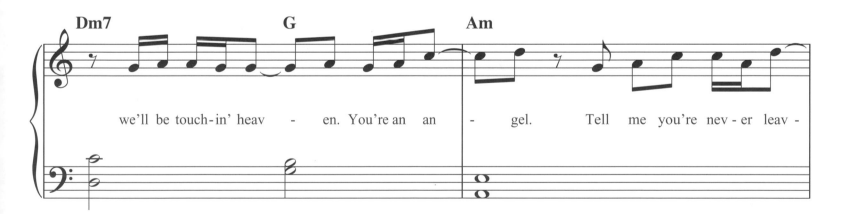

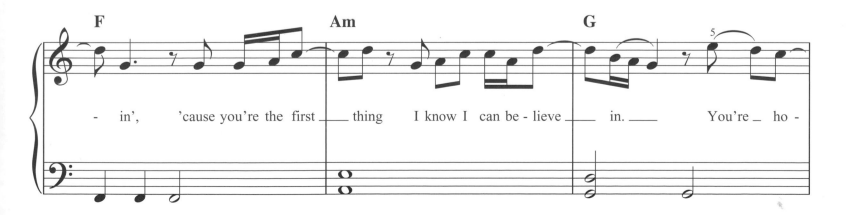

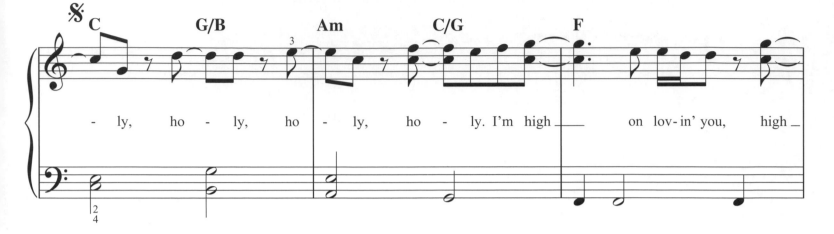

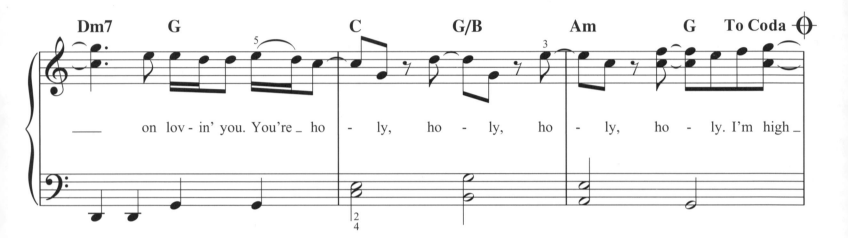

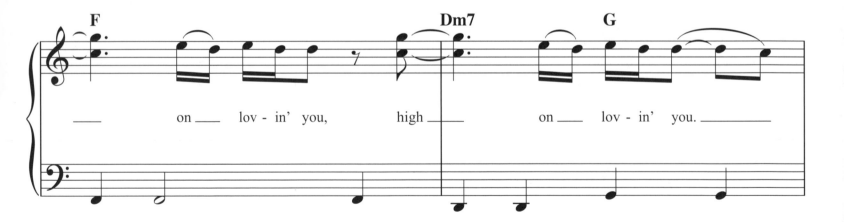

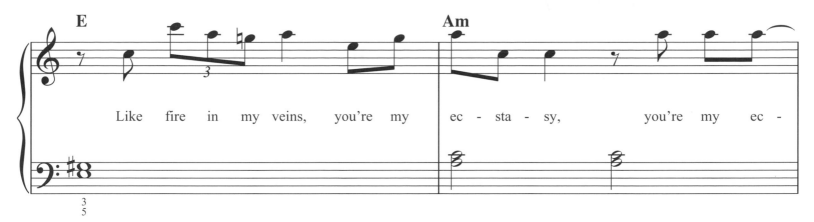

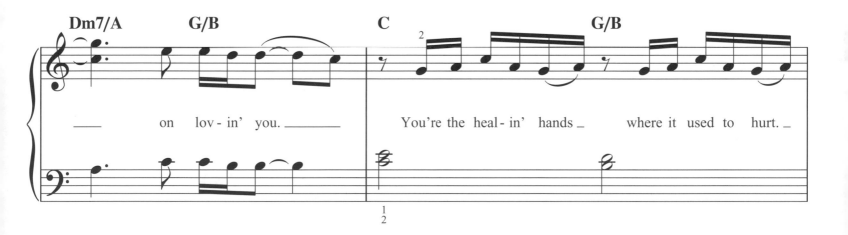

# I DON'T WANNA LIVE FOREVER

(Fifty Shades Darker)

from FIFTY SHADES DARKER

Words and Music by TAYLOR SWIFT,
JACK ANTONOFF and SAM DEW

**Easy Pop feel**

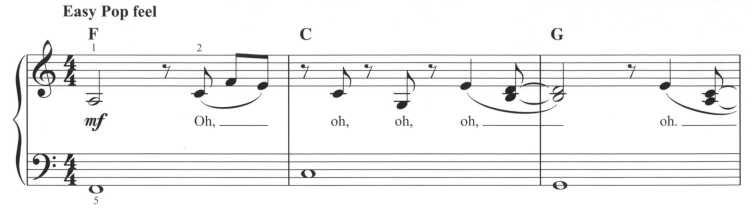

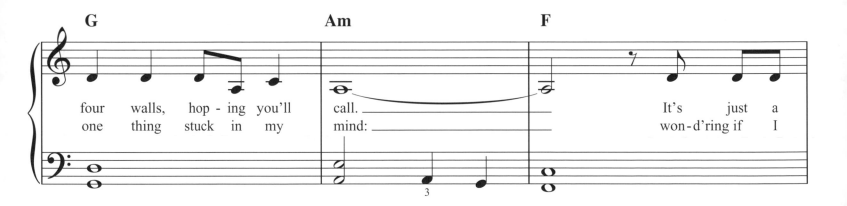

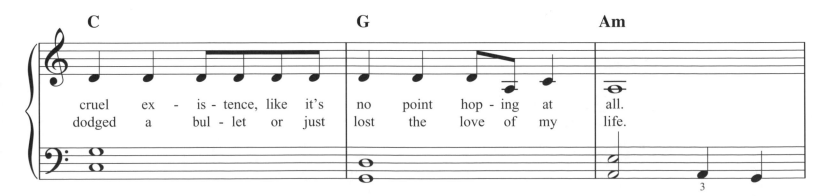

65

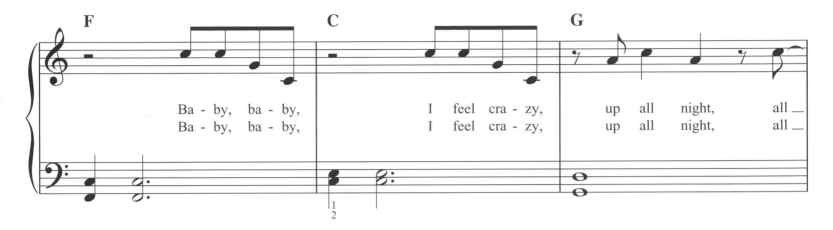

- er. I just wan-na keep call-ing your name ___ un-til you come back

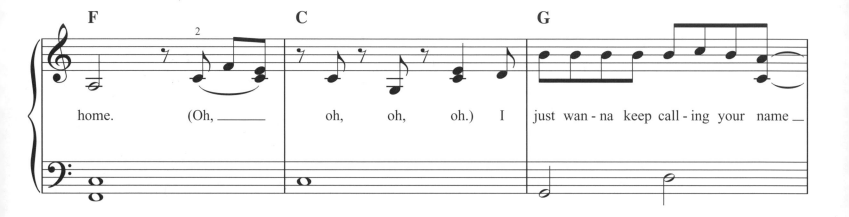

home. (Oh, ___ oh, oh, oh.) I just wan-na keep call-ing your name ___

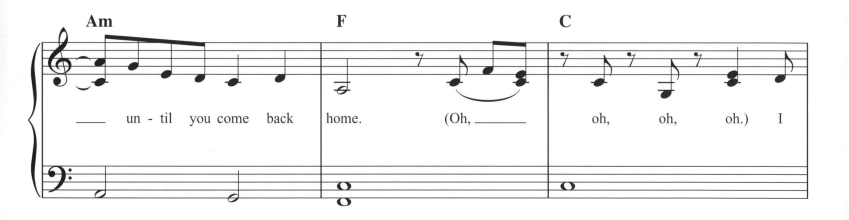

___ un-til you come back home. (Oh, ___ oh, oh, oh.) I

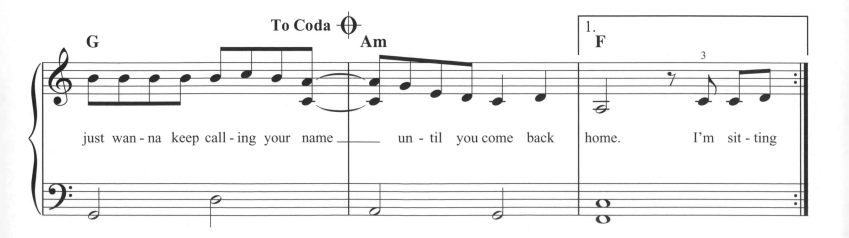

just wan-na keep call-ing your name ___ un-til you come back home. I'm sit-ting

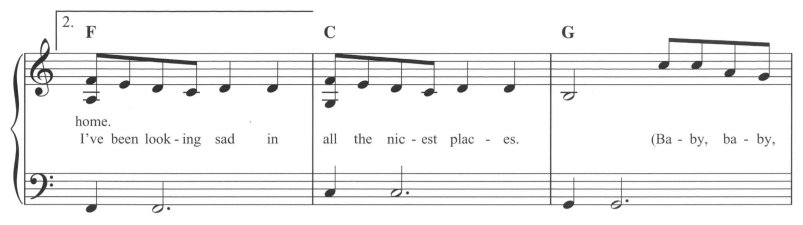

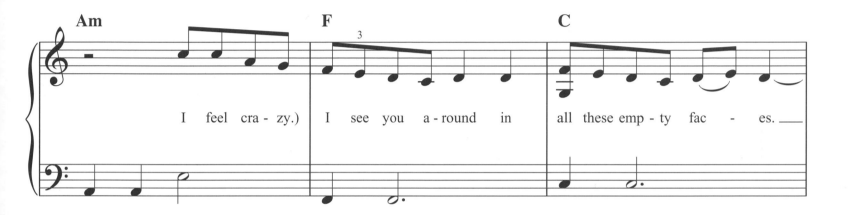

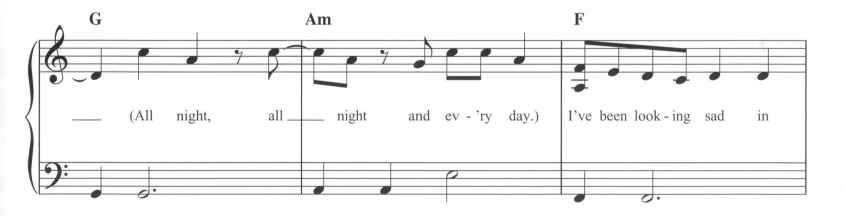

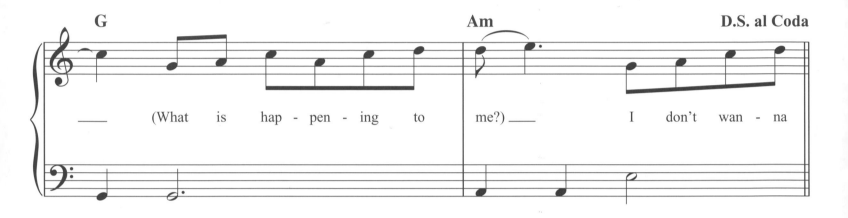

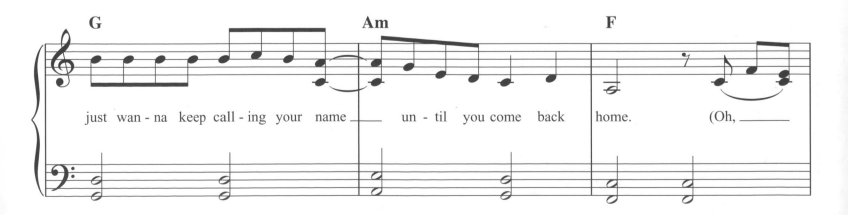

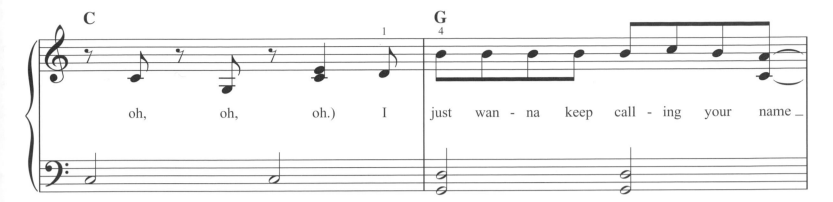

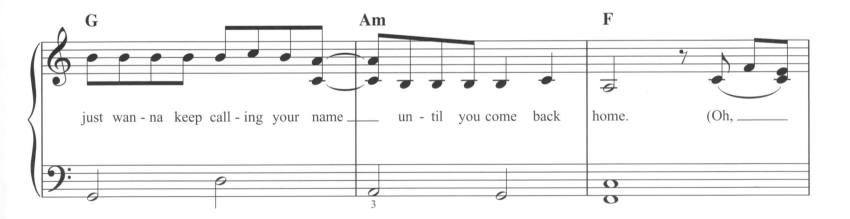

# LOVE ON THE WEEKEND

Words and Music by
JOHN MAYER

It's a Fri - day;
You be the D. J.,

we fi - n'lly made it. I can't be - lieve I get to see ___ your face. ___
I'll be the driv - er. You put your feet up in the get - a - way car. ___

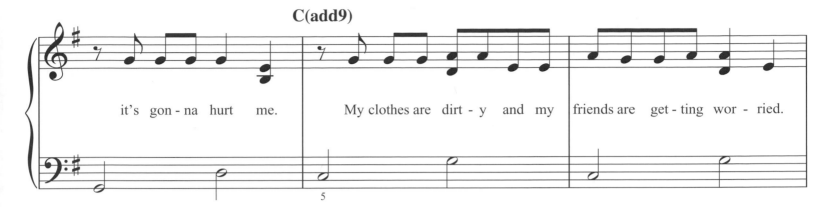

love on the week - end, __ I'm bust-ed up, but I'm lov-ing ev-'ry min-ute of it.

Love on __ the week - end. __

Love on __ the week - end. __

# MERCY

Words and Music by SHAWN MENDES,
TEDDY GEIGER, DANNY PARKER
and ILSEY JUBER

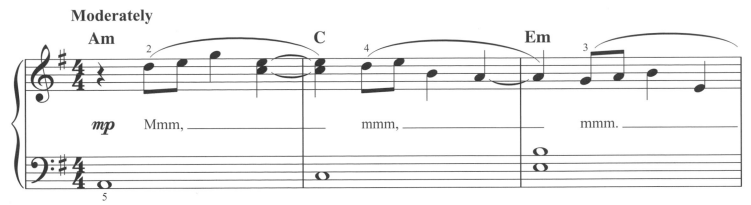

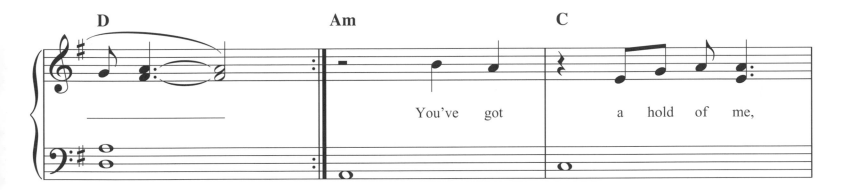

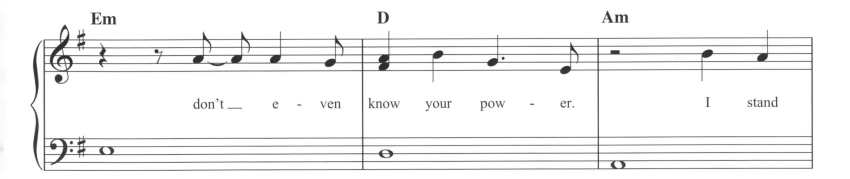

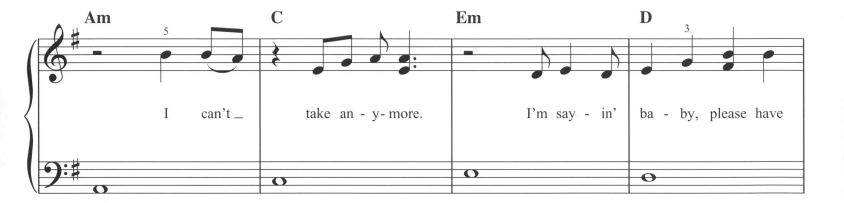

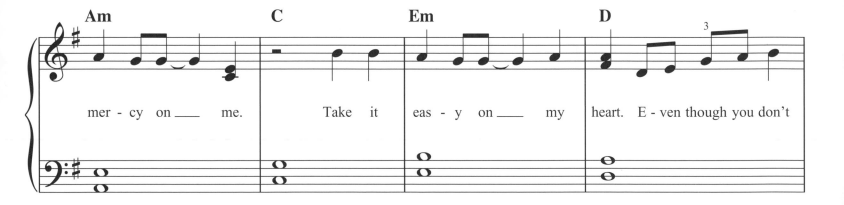

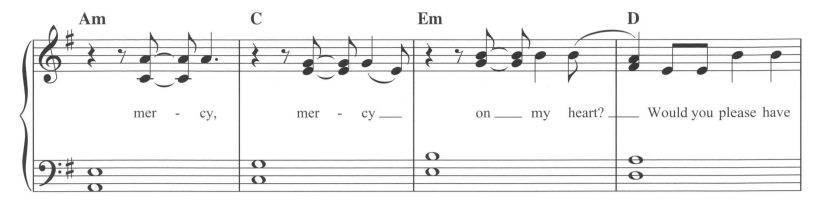

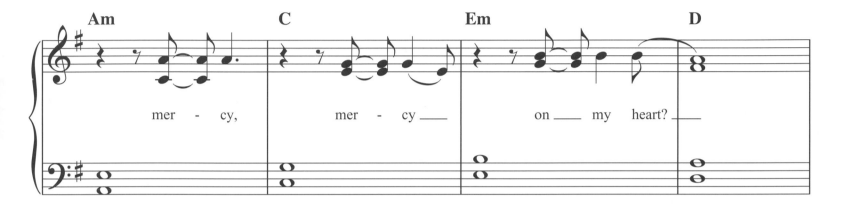

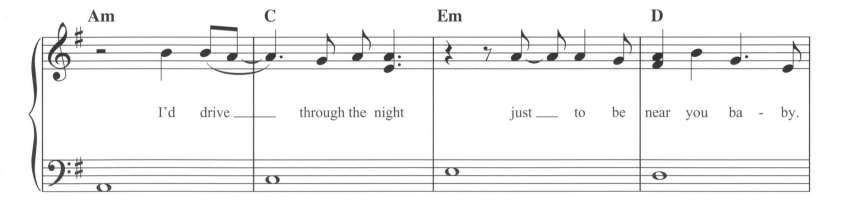

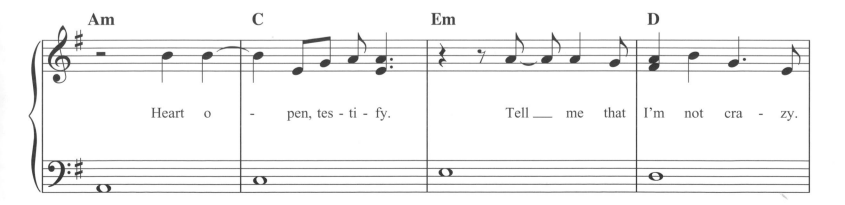

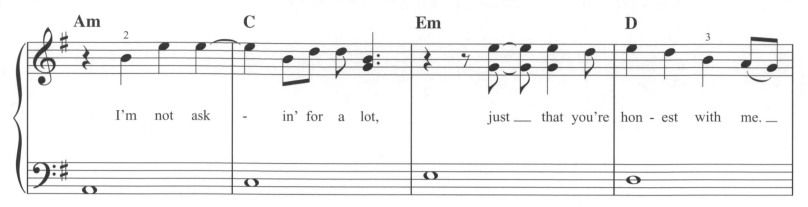

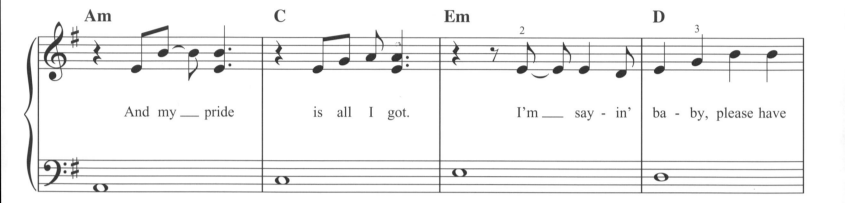

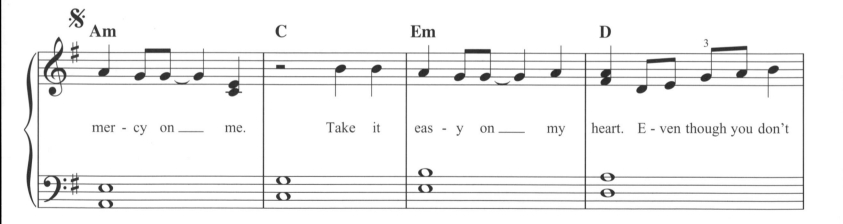

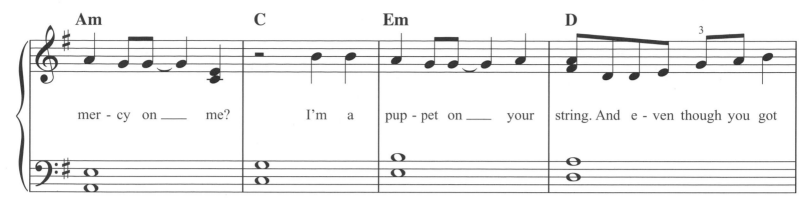

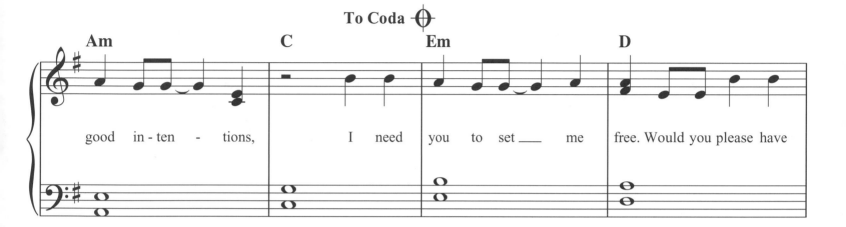

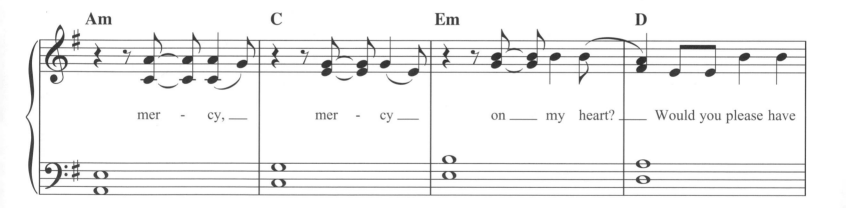

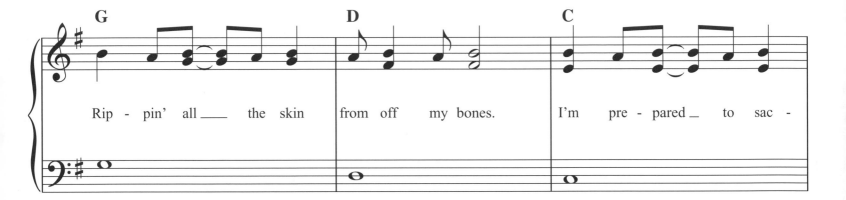

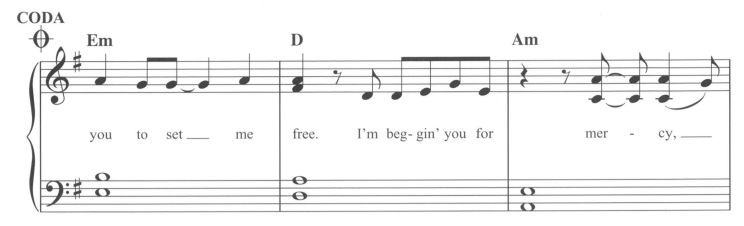

# MILLION REASONS

Words and Music by STEFANI GERMANOTTA,
MARK RONSON and HILLARY LINDSEY

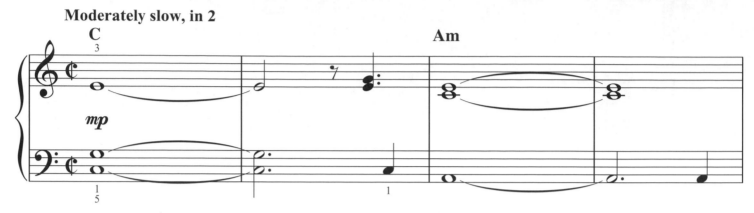

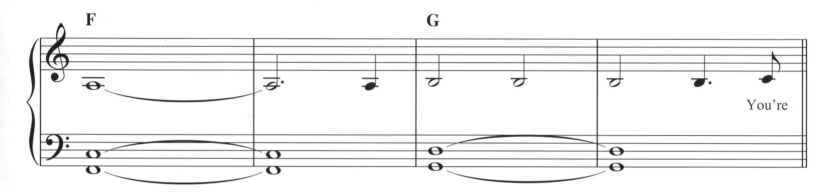

giv- in' me a mil-lion rea-sons to let you go. ___ You're giv- in' me a mil-lion rea-sons
Head stuck in a cy-cle, I look off and I stare. ___ It's like that I've stopped breath-in' but com-

to quit the show. ___ You're giv- in' me a mil-lion rea-sons, give me a mil-lion rea-sons.
plete-ly a- ware. ___ 'Cause you're giv- in' me a mil-lion rea-sons, give me a mil-lion rea-sons.

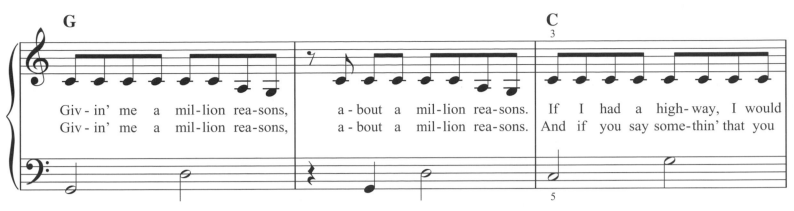

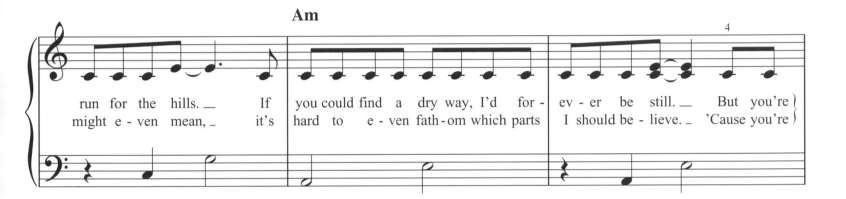

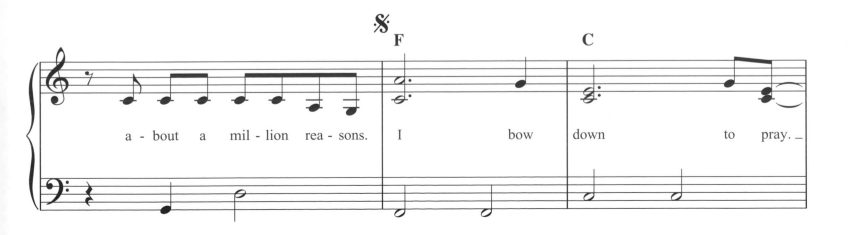

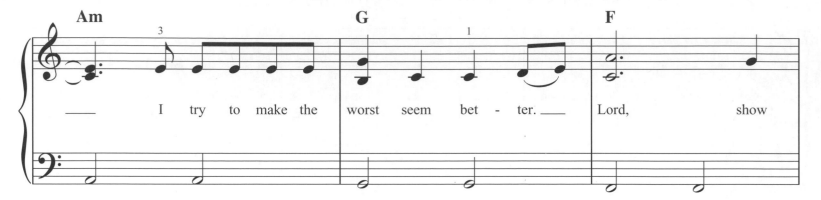

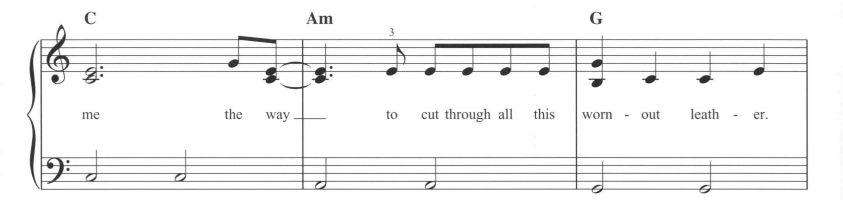

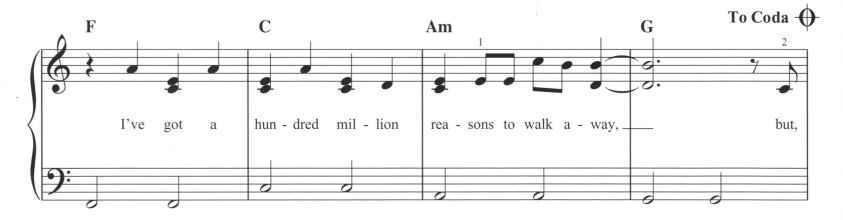

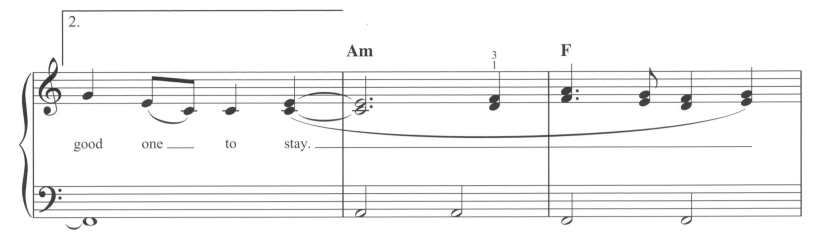

**2.**

**Am** **F**

good one ___ to stay. ___

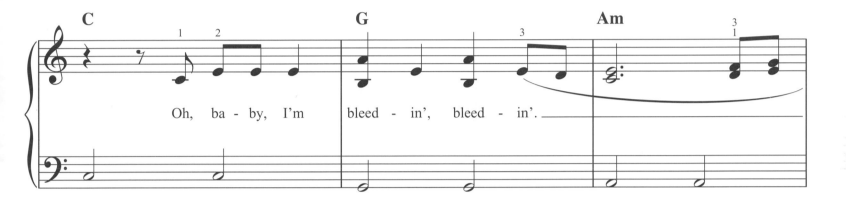

**C** **G** **Am**

Oh, ba - by, I'm bleed - in', bleed - in'. ___

**F** **C** **G**

Can't you give me what I'm need - in', need - in'?

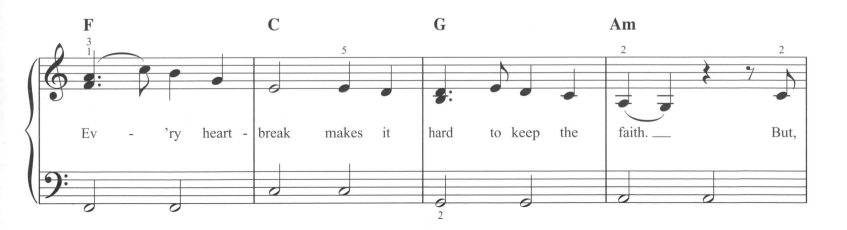

**F** **C** **G** **Am**

Ev - 'ry heart - break makes it hard to keep the faith. ___ But,

ba - by, I just need one good one, good one, good one, good one,

**D.S. al Coda**

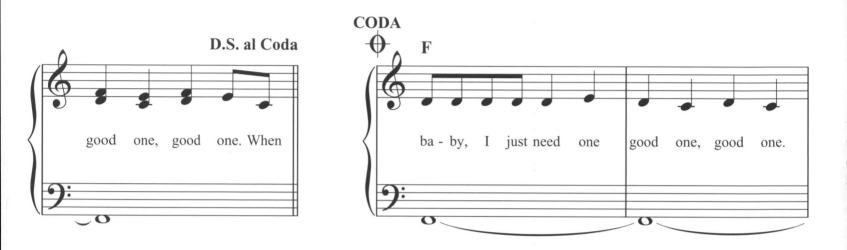

good one, good one. When

**CODA**

**F**

ba - by, I just need one good one, good one.

Tell me that you'll be the good one, good one. Ba - by, I just need one

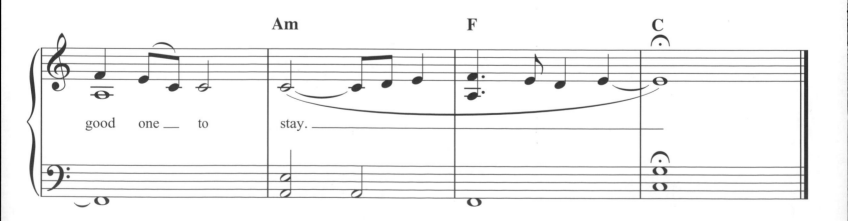

good one _ to stay. _

**Am**          **F**          **C**

# RIDE

Words and Music by
TYLER JOSEPH

I just wan-na stay in the sun where I find,

_ I know it's hard some-times, _ piec-es of peace

in the sun's peace of mind. _ I know it's hard some-times. _

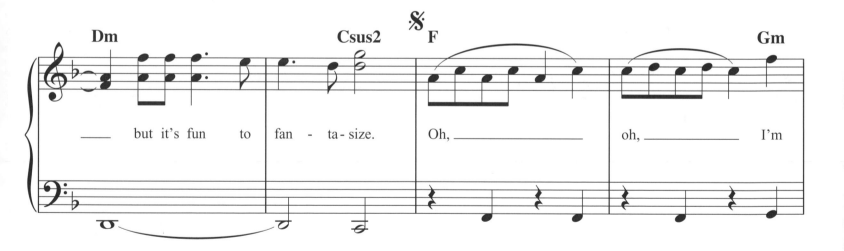

Oh, _____ I'm fall - ing, so I'm tak - ing my time on my

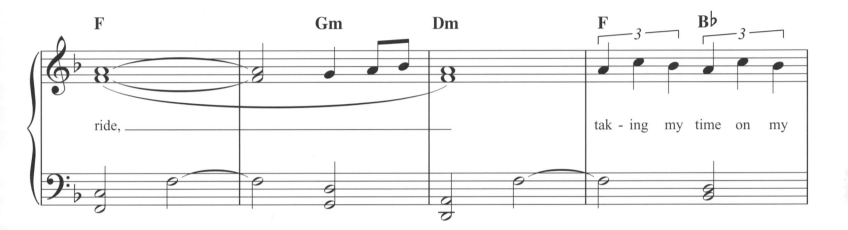

ride, _____ tak - ing my time on my

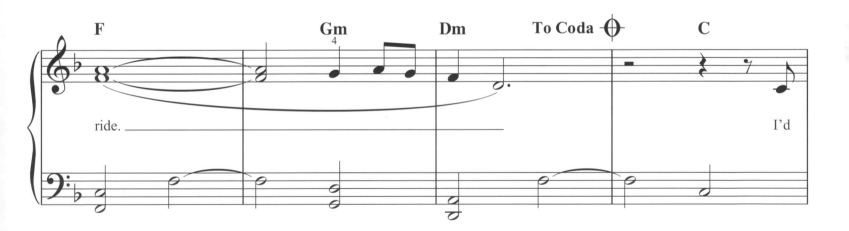

ride. _____ I'd

die for you. That's eas - y to say. We have a list of peo - ple that we would take a

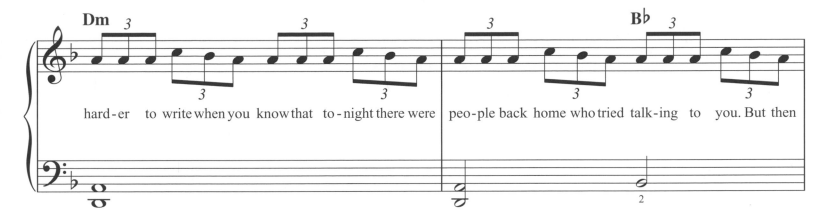

hard-er to write when you know that to-night there were peo-ple back home who tried talk-ing to you. But then

you ig-nored them still. ___ All these ques-tions, they're for real, like who would you

live for, who would you die for, and would you ev-er kill? ___

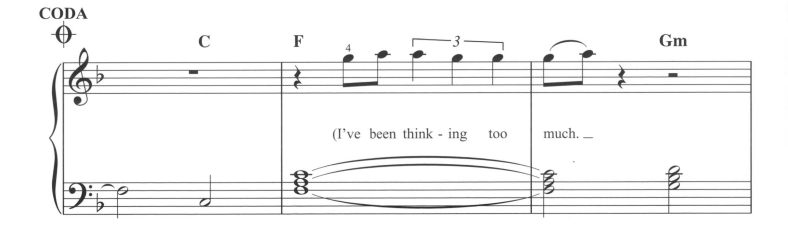

(I've been think-ing too much. ___

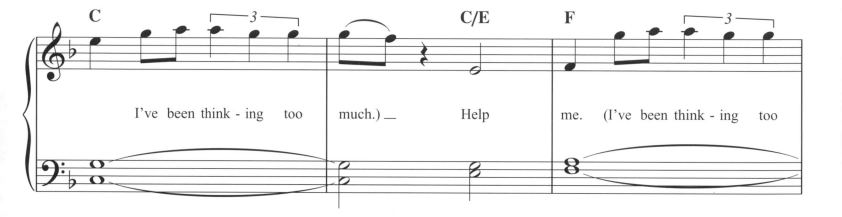

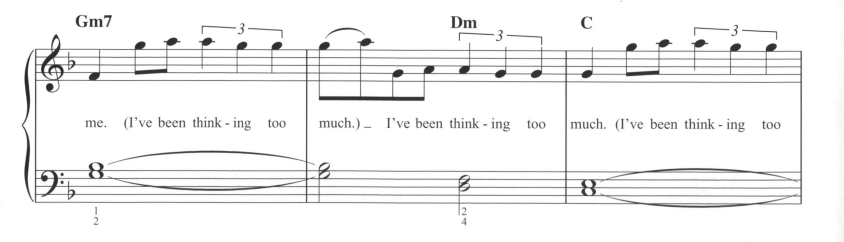

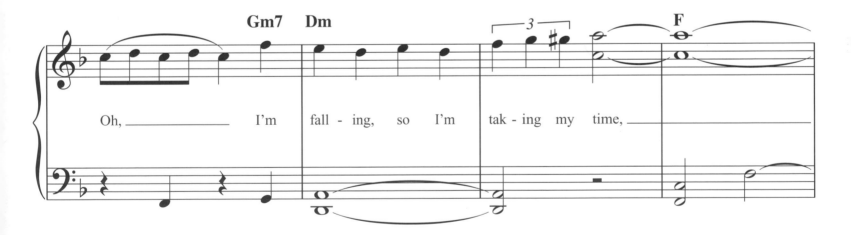

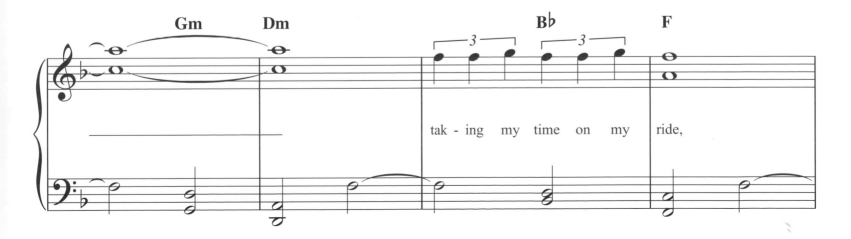

whoa, oh, oh.

Oh, _____

oh, _____ I'm fall - ing, so I'm tak - ing my time on my

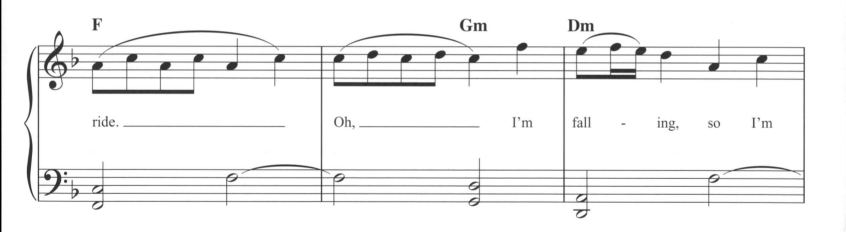

ride. _____ Oh, _____ I'm fall - ing, so I'm

tak - ing my time on my... I've been think-ing too much.

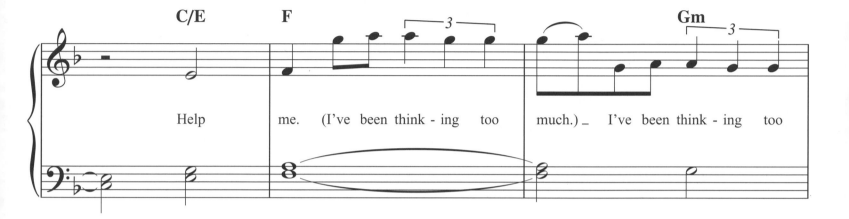

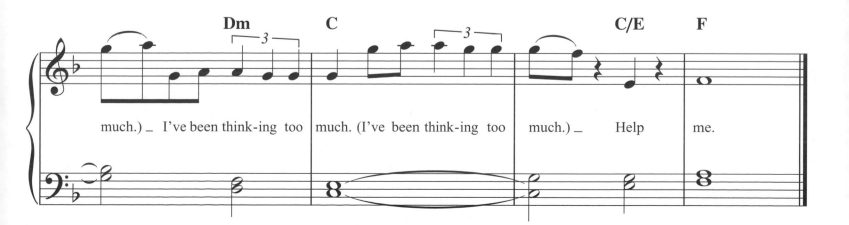

# OPHELIA

Words and Music by JEREMY FRAITES
and WESLEY SCHULTZ

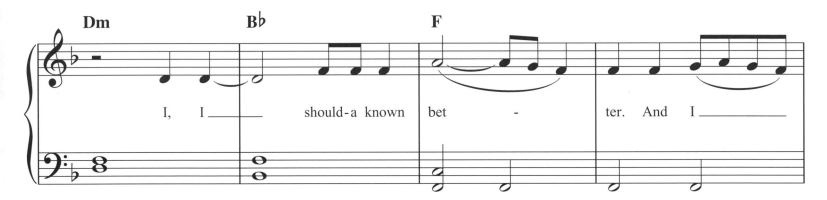

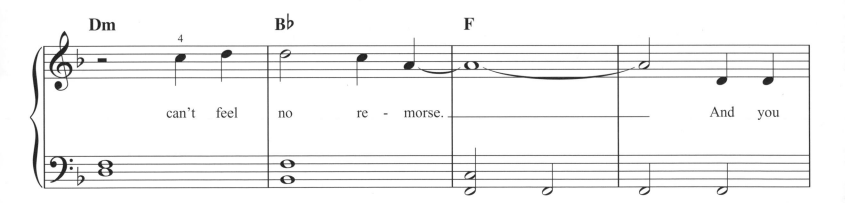

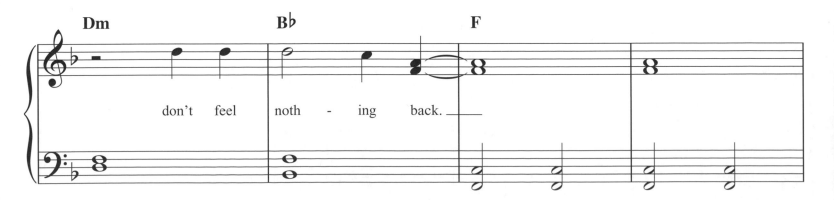

I, I've __ got a new girl - friend. She

feels like __ he's on top. __ And I __

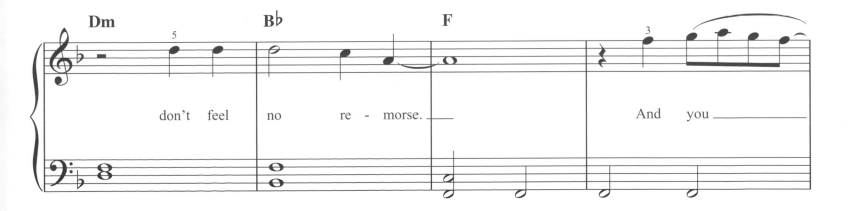

don't feel no re - morse. __ And you __

can't see  past  my  blind  -  ness.

Oh,  O - phe - li - a, _____  you've been on my  mind, girl, since  the  flood. _

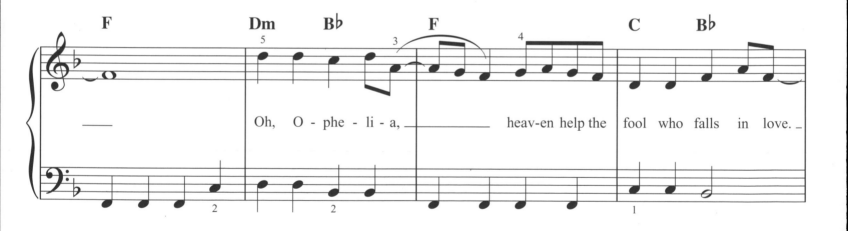

_____  Oh,  O - phe - li - a, _____  heav-en help the  fool  who falls  in  love. _

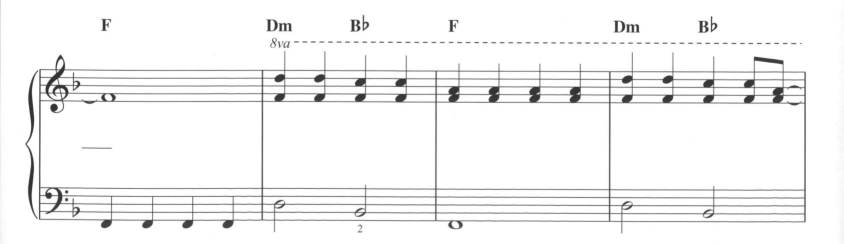

_____

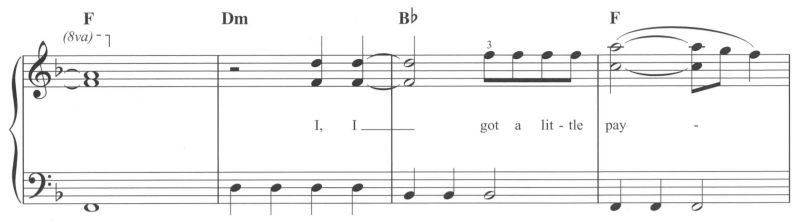

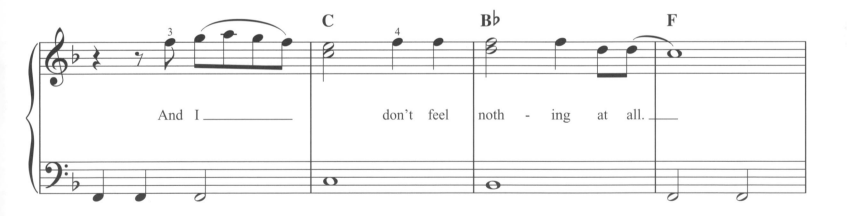

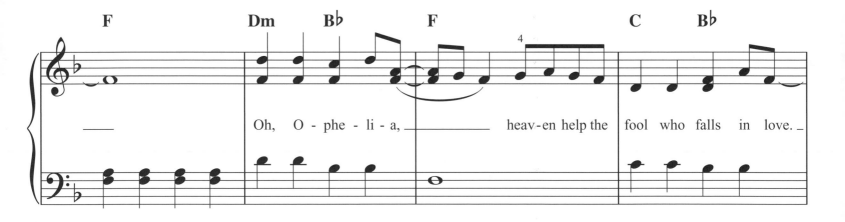

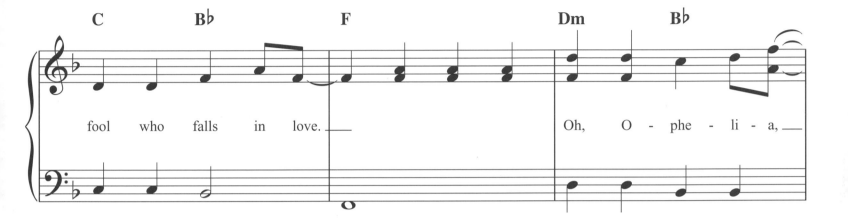

# PLAY THAT SONG

Words and Music by HOAGY CARMICHAEL,
FRANK LOESSER, PAT MONAHAN
and WILLIAM WIIK LARSEN

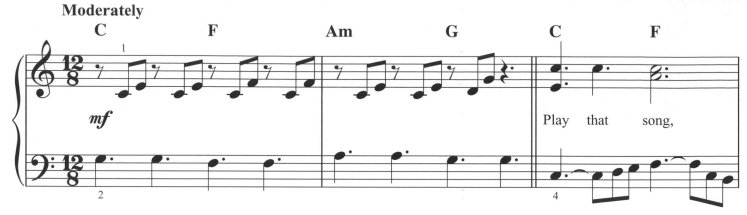

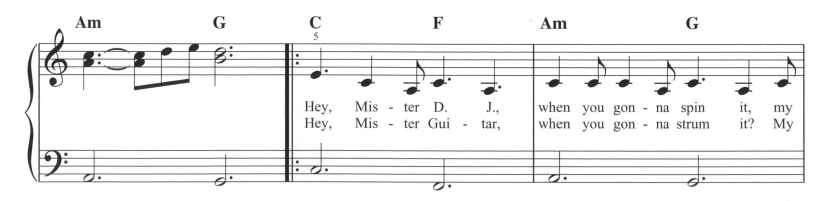

ba - by's fa - v'rite rec - ord? She been waiting for a min - ute. She in
girl just heard this song and you should play it 'cause she loves it. Can you

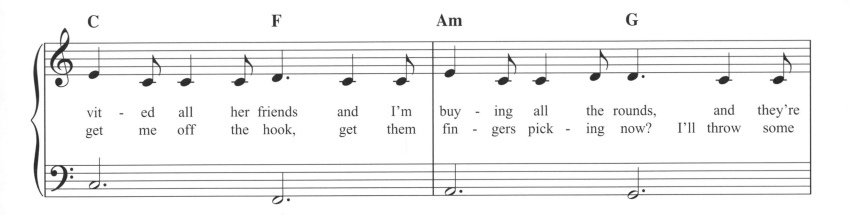

vit - ed all her friends and I'm buy - ing all the rounds, and they're
get me off the hook, get them fin - gers pick - ing now? I'll throw some

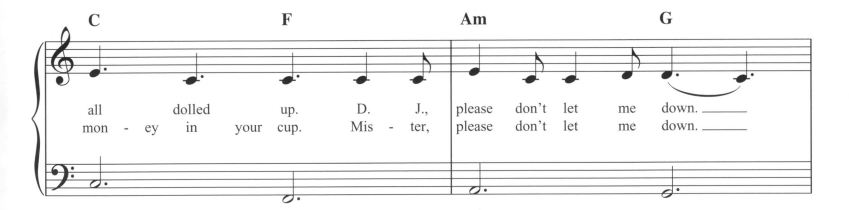

all dolled up. D. J., please don't let me down. _____
mon - ey in your cup. Mis - ter, please don't let me down. _____

When you gon - na play __ that song now? When you gon - na earn __ that pay?
When you gon - na play __ that song now? Why you got - ta hes - i - tate?

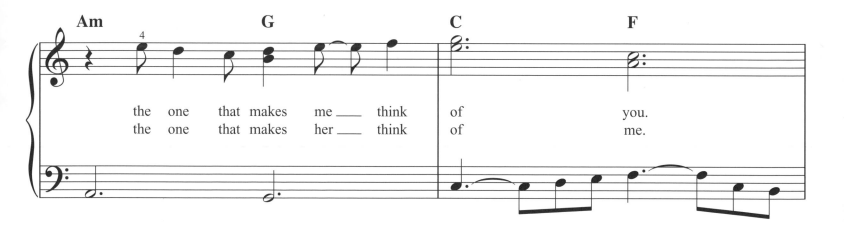

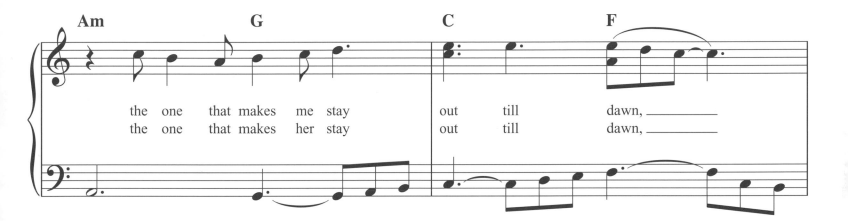

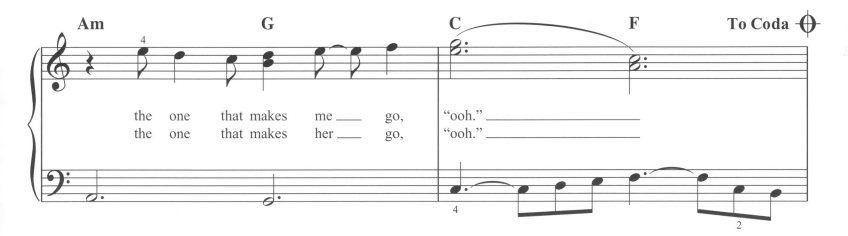

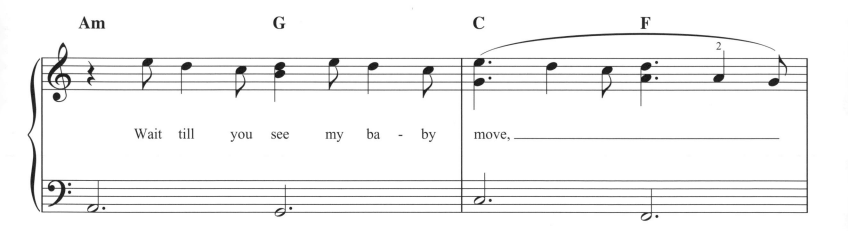

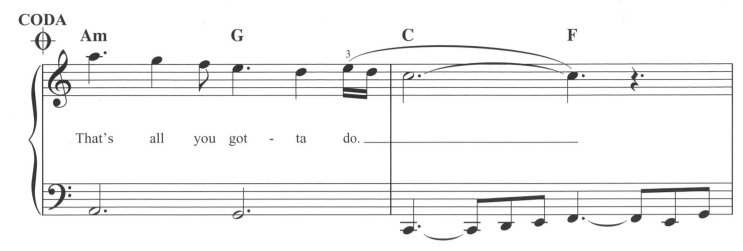

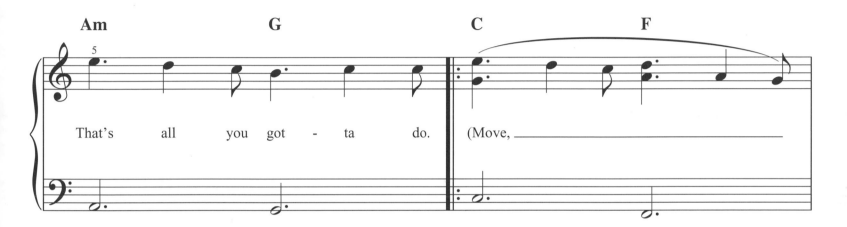

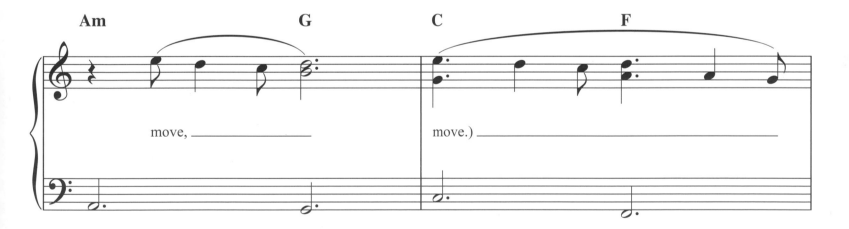

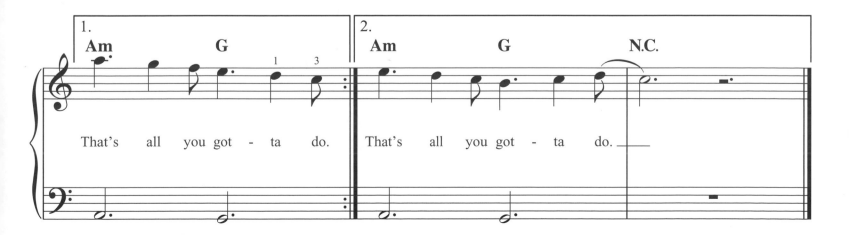

# RUNNIN'
## from HIDDEN FIGURES

Words and Music by
PHARRELL WILLIAMS

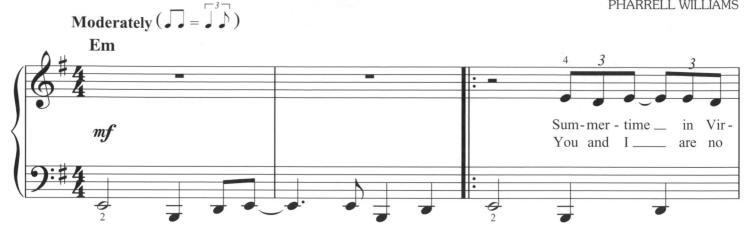

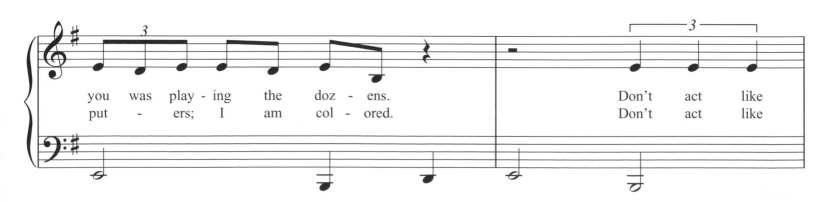

you was there — when you was-n't

I know they — say, "Crawl 'fore you walk,"

but in my — mind I al - read - y jog.

If I stand — still, I

can - not get far.

They want the moon; I'm on Mars. —

Some - times my mind

F#7

F

Em

dives

deep

when I'm run - nin'. —

I don't want no free

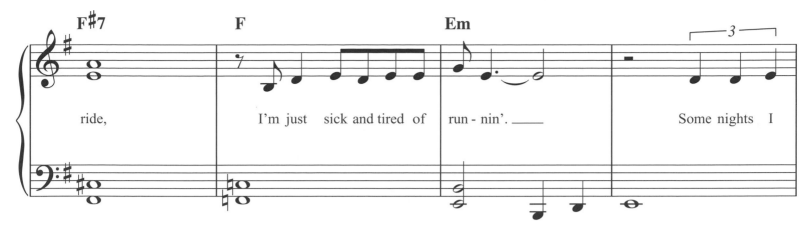

ride, I'm just sick and tired of run - nin'. _____ Some nights I

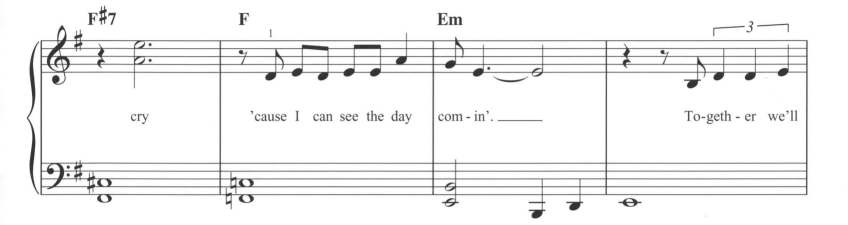

cry 'cause I can see the day com - in'. _____ To-geth - er we'll

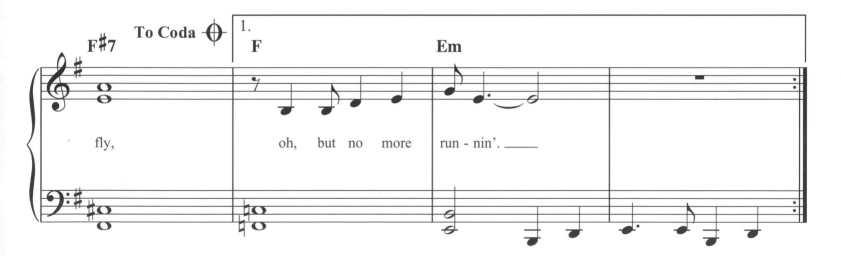

fly, oh, but no more run - nin'. _____

oh, but no more run - nin'.

112

**D.S. al Coda**

**CODA**

F

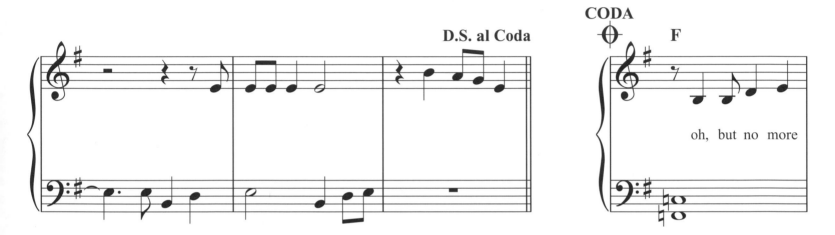

oh, but no more

**Em**

run-nin', no.

1.

2.

# SHAPE OF YOU

Words and Music by ED SHEERAN,
KEVIN BRIGGS, KANDI BURRUSS,
TAMEKA COTTLE, STEVE MAC
and JOHNNY McDAID

**Moderately**

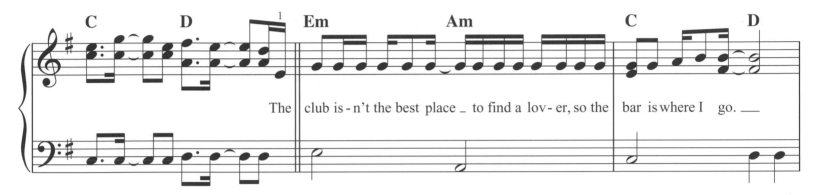

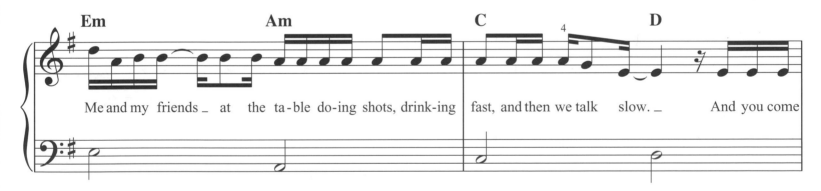

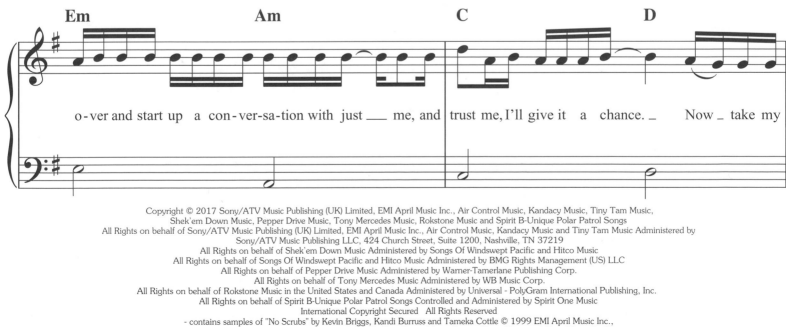

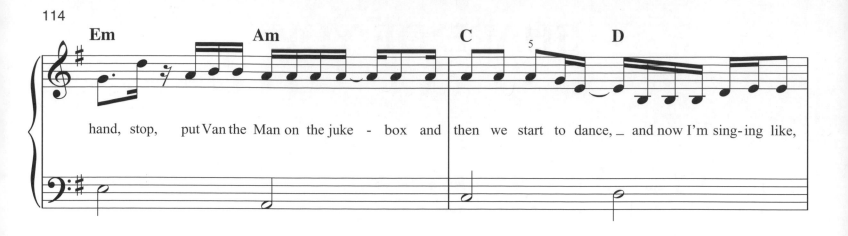

hand, stop, put Van the Man on the juke - box and then we start to dance, __ and now I'm sing-ing like,

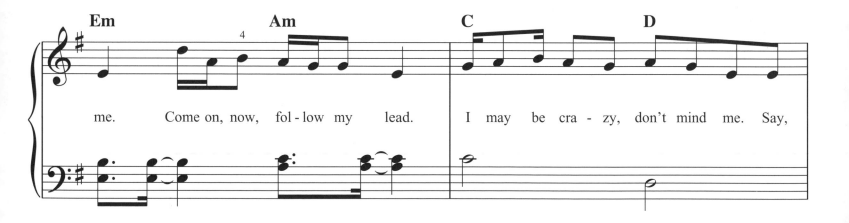

girl, you know I want your love. Your love was hand-made for some-bod-y like __

me. Come on, now, fol-low my lead. I may be cra-zy, don't mind me. Say,

boy, let's not talk too much. Grab on my waist and put that bod-y on __

me. Come on, now, fol - low my lead. Come, come on, now, fol - low my lead. Mmm. _____

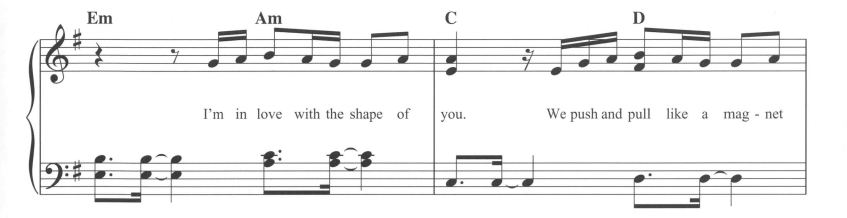

I'm in love with the shape of you. We push and pull like a mag - net

do. Al - though my heart is fall - ing, too, I'm in love with your bod - y.

Last night you were in my room, and now my bed - sheets smell like

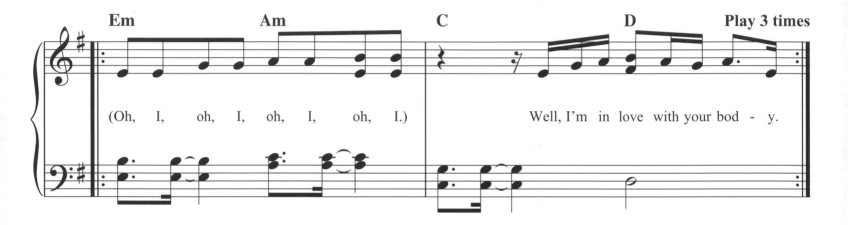

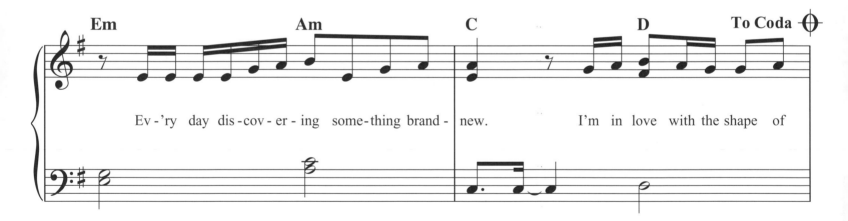

me are thrift - y, so go "all you can eat," __ fill up your bag and I fill up a plate. We talk for

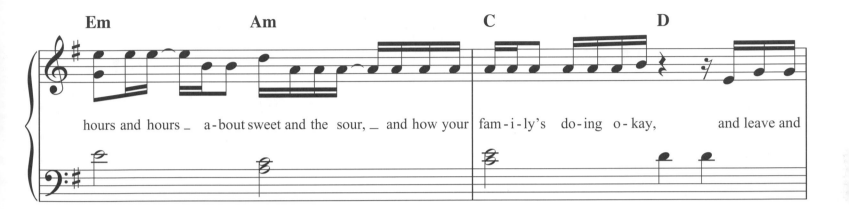

hours and hours __ a-bout sweet and the sour, __ and how your fam-i-ly's do-ing o-kay, and leave and

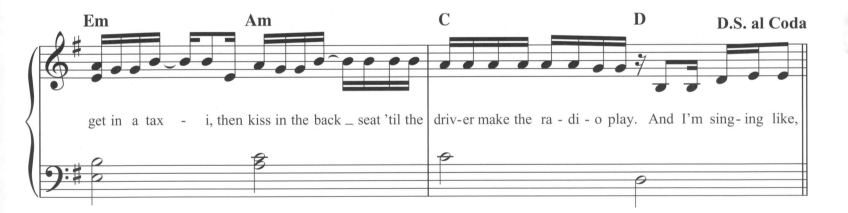

get in a tax - i, then kiss in the back __ seat 'til the driv-er make the ra-di-o play. And I'm sing-ing like,

you. Come on, __ be my ba - by, come on. Come on, __ be my ba - by, come on.

Come on, ___ be my ba-by, come on.　Come on, ___ be my ba-by, come on.　Come on, ___ be my ba-by, come on.

Come on, ___ be my ba-by, come on.　Come on, ___ be my ba-by, come on.　Come on, ___ be my ba-by, come on.

I'm in love with the shape of　you.　We push and pull like a mag-net

do.　Al-though my heart is fall-ing, too,　I'm in love with your bod-y.

Last night you were in my room, and now my bed-sheets smell like you. Ev-'ry day dis-cov-er-ing some-thing brand - new. Well, I'm in love with your bod - y.

(Come on, __ be my ba - by, come on. Come on.) __ I'm in love with your bod - y.

**Play 3 times**

Ev-'ry day dis-cov-er-ing some-thing brand- new. I'm in love with the shape of you.

# SAY YOU WON'T LET GO

Words and Music by STEVEN SOLOMON,
JAMES ARTHUR and NEIL ORMANDY

Moderately

I met you in the dark,
I wake you up with some

you lit me up,
break-fast in bed,

you made me feel   as though
I'll bring you cof-fee with

I was e - nough. _
a kiss on your head. __

We danced the night  a - way,
I'll take the kids  to school,

we drank too _ much,
wave them good - bye.

I held your hair back when
I'll thank my luck - y  stars

you were throw-ing up. ____
for _ that _ night. ___

Then you smiled    o - ver your shoul - der    for   a  min-ute, I  was stone cold  so - ber.
When you looked    o - ver  your  shoul - der    for  a  min-ute I  for - get  I'm  old - er.

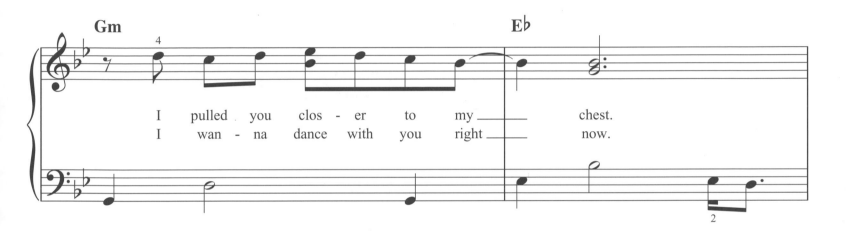

I   pulled   you  clos - er   to    my _____    chest.
I   wan - na  dance  with   you   right _____   now.

And you asked     me  to stay   o - ver,     I said, I         al - rea - dy  told  ya
And you look  as  beau-ti-ful  as  ev - er     and  I swear that ev-'ry day you'll get  bet - ter,

I   think   that    you  should  get   some _____   rest.
you make  me   feel   this   way   some    -    how.

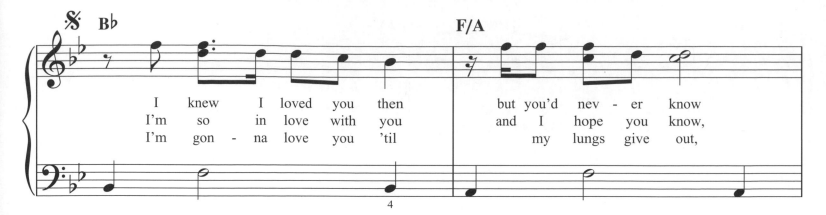

I knew I loved you then
I'm so in love with you
I'm gon - na love you 'til

but you'd nev - er know
and I hope you know,
my lungs give out,

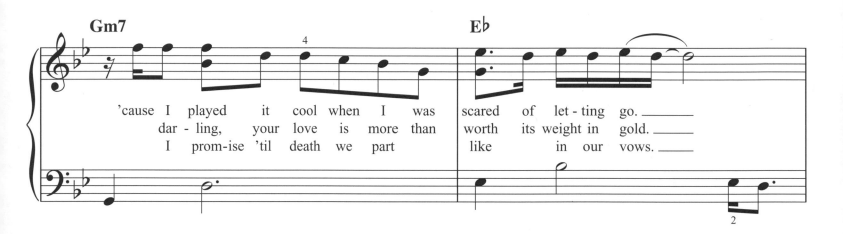

'cause I played it cool when I was
dar - ling, your love is more than
I prom - ise 'til death we part

scared of let - ting go.
worth its weight in gold.
like in our vows.

I know I need - ed you
We've come so far my dear,
So I wrote this song for you,

but I nev - er showed,
look how we've grown
now ev - 'ry - bod - y knows

and I wan - na stay with you un-
and I wan - na stay with you un-
that it's just you and me un-

til we're grey and old.
til we're grey and old.
til we're grey and old.

Just say you won't let go.

Just

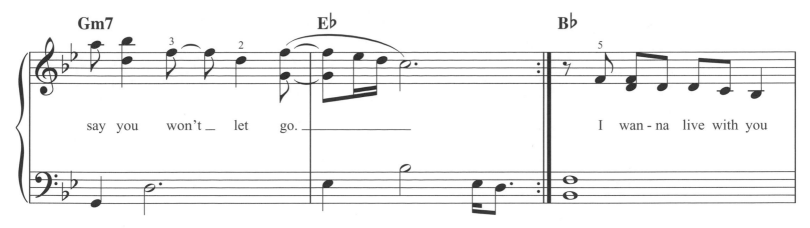

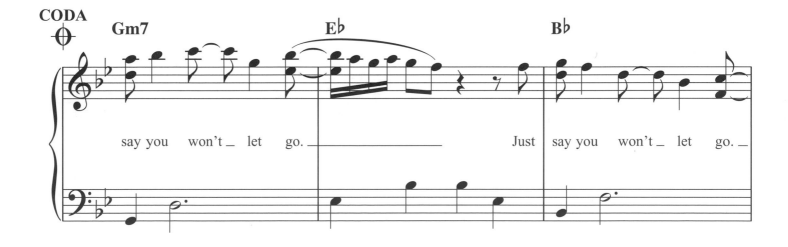

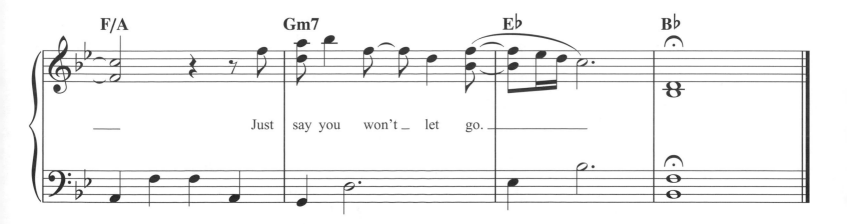

# 7 YEARS

Words and Music by LUKAS FORCHHAMMER,
MORTEN RISTORP, STEFAN FORREST,
DAVID LABREL, CHRISTOPHER BROWN
and MORTEN PILEGAARD

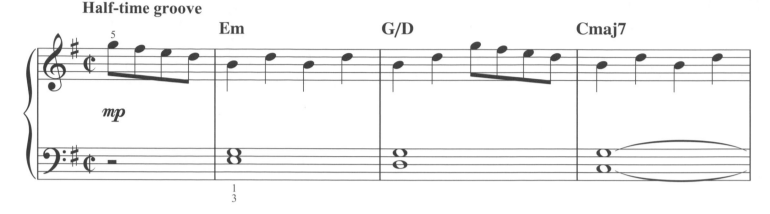

Once I was sev-en years old, my ma-ma told

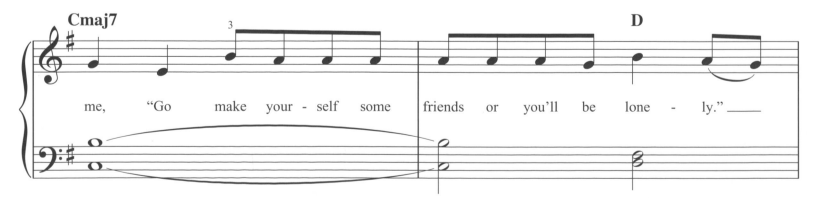

me, "Go make your-self some friends or you'll be lone-ly." ___

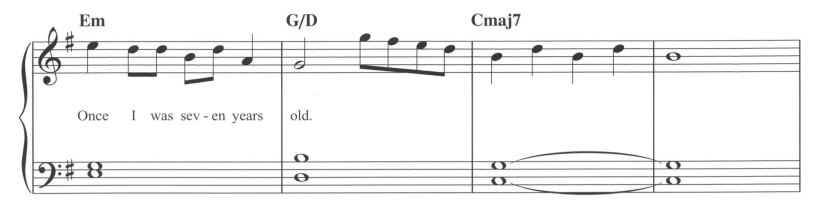

Once    I   was sev - en years   old.

It   was   a   big,  big   world, but   we thought we were big - ger.   Push-ing each oth - er   to   the

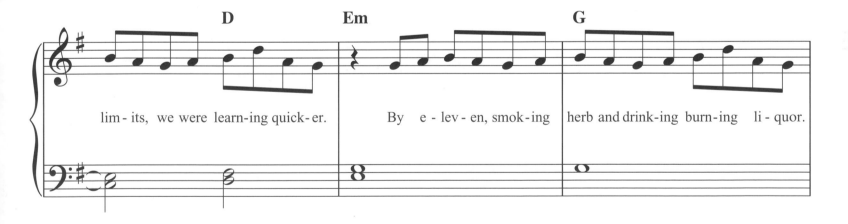

lim - its,  we were learn-ing quick-er.   By   e - lev - en, smok-ing   herb and drink-ing burn-ing   li - quor.

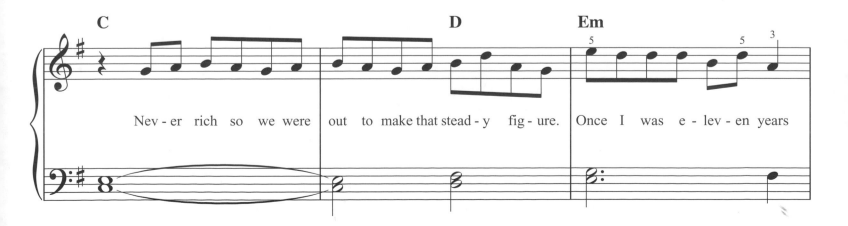

Nev - er  rich  so  we were   out  to make that stead - y   fig - ure.   Once  I  was  e - lev - en years

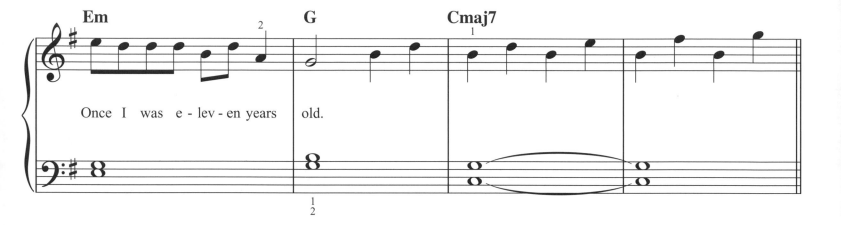

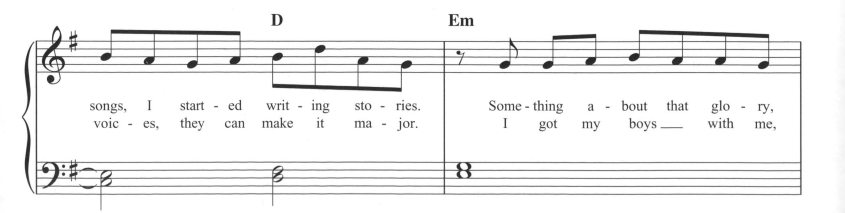

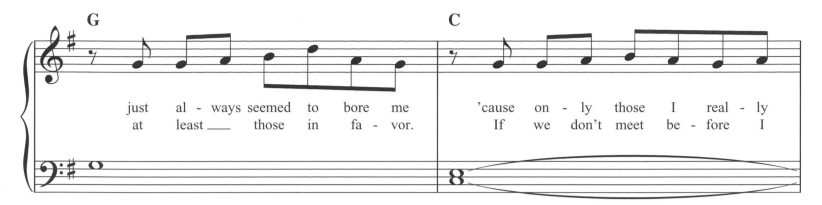

just  al - ways seemed to  bore  me
at  least ___ those  in  fa - vor.

'cause  on - ly  those  I  real - ly
If  we  don't  meet  be - fore  I

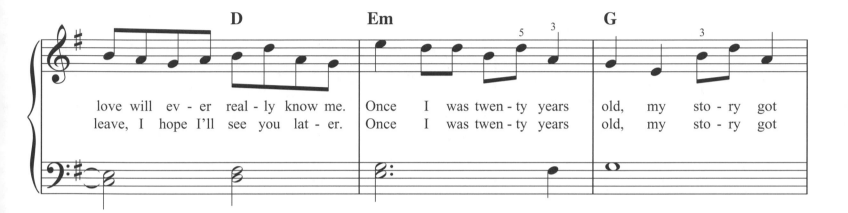

love will ev - er  real - ly know me.
leave, I hope I'll see you lat - er.

Once  I  was twen - ty years
Once  I  was twen - ty years

old,  my  sto - ry  got
old,  my  sto - ry  got

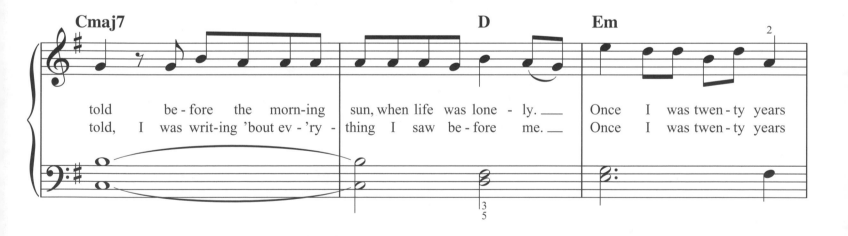

told  be - fore  the  morn - ing
told,  I  was writ - ing 'bout ev - 'ry -

sun, when life was lone - ly. ___
thing I saw be - fore me. ___

Once  I  was twen - ty years
Once  I  was twen - ty years

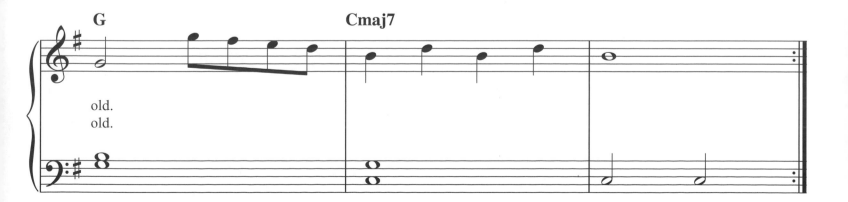

old.
old.

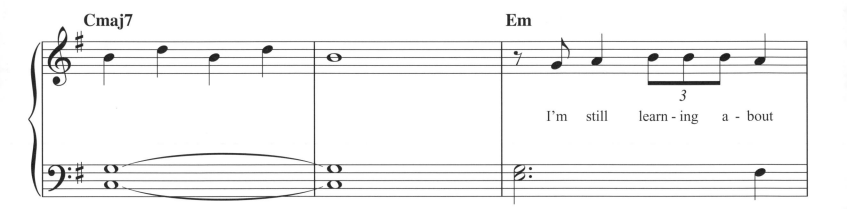

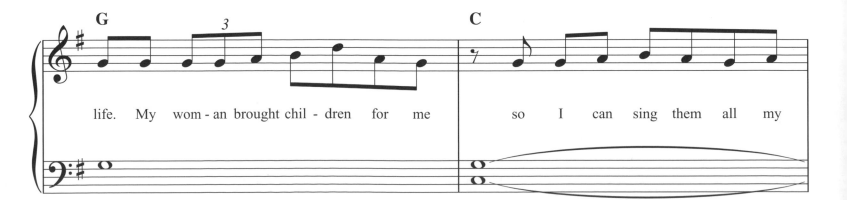

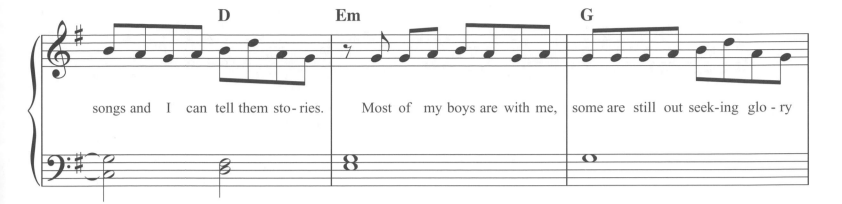

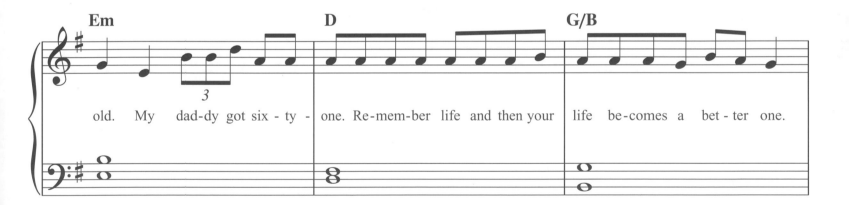

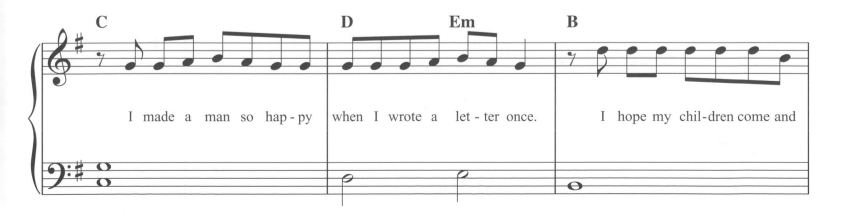

vis - it once or twice a month. Soon I'll be six - ty years old. Will I think the world is

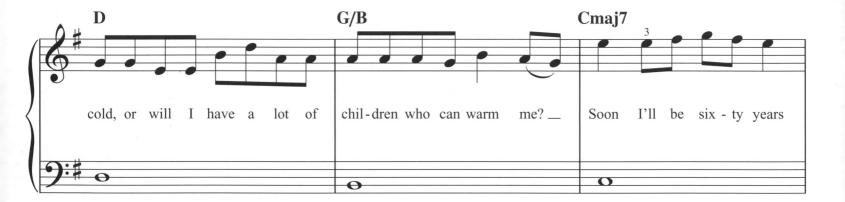

cold, or will I have a lot of chil-dren who can warm me? __ Soon I'll be six - ty years

old. Soon I'll be six - ty years

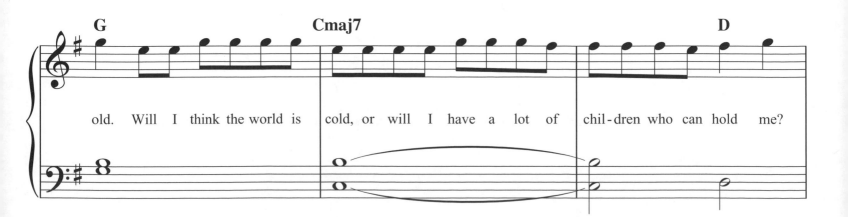

old. Will I think the world is cold, or will I have a lot of chil-dren who can hold me?

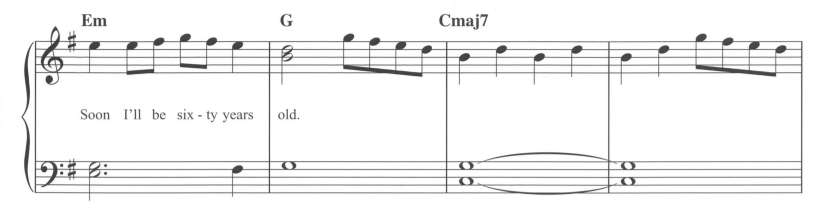

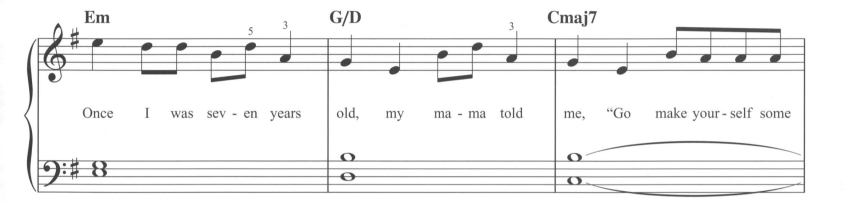

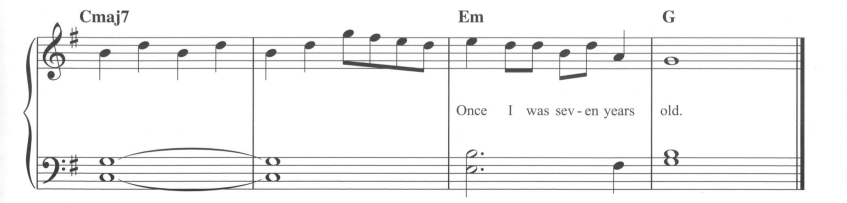

# SHAKE IT OFF

Words and Music by TAYLOR SWIFT,
MAX MARTIN and SHELLBACK

at least, that's what peo - ple say, _____ mm, mm. That's what peo - ple
And that's what they don't know, _____ mm, mm. That's what they don't

**Am**

say, _____ mm, mm. But I keep cruis - ing;
know, _____ mm, mm. But I keep cruis - ing;

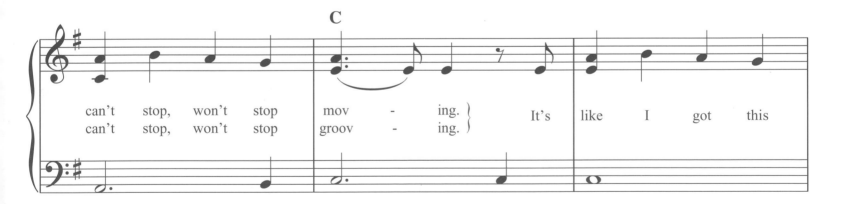

**C**

can't stop, won't stop mov - ing. } It's like I got this
can't stop, won't stop groov - ing. }

**G**

mu - sic in my mind say - ing, "It's gon - na be al - right." _

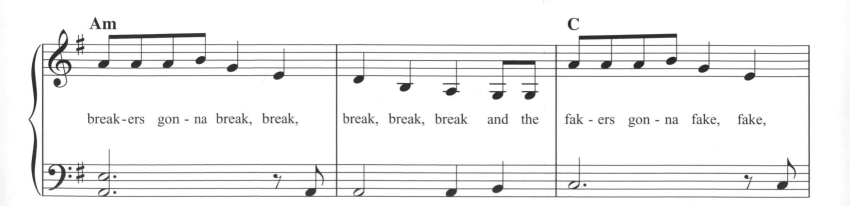

fake, fake, fake, ba - by. I'm just gon - na shake, shake, shake, shake, shake; \_ I

shake it off, I shake it off. I nev - er miss a off. (Ooh, \_ ooh!) I

shake it off, I shake it off. I, I, I shake it off, I shake it

off. I, I, I shake it off, I shake it off. I, I, I

shake it off, I shake it off. (Ooh, _ ooh!)

**N.C.**

1. *Spoken: (See additional lyrics)*
2. Rap: *(See additional lyrics)*

*Rap ends* Yeah, _ oh. _____ 'Cause the

**D.S. al Coda**

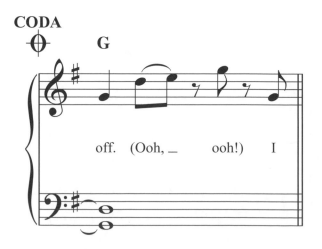

**CODA** **G**

off. (Ooh, _ ooh!) I

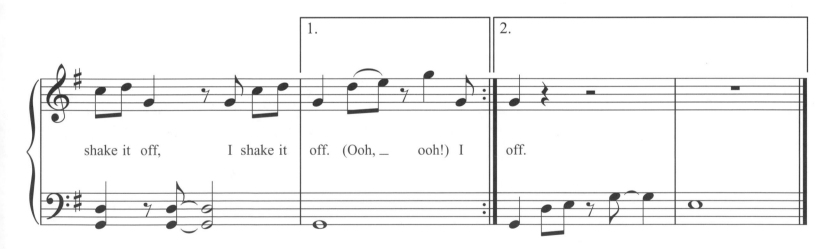

*Additional Lyrics*

*Spoken: Hey, hey, hey! Just think: While you've been getting*
*Down and out about the liars and the dirty, dirty*
*Cheats of the world, you could've been getting down to*
*This. Sick. Beat!*

**Rap:** My ex-man brought his new girlfriend.
She's like, "Oh, my god!" But I'm just gonna shake.
And to the fella over there with the hella good hair,
Won't you come on over, baby? We can shake, shake, shake.

# SHE USED TO BE MINE
## from WAITRESS THE MUSICAL

Words and Music by
SARA BAREILLES

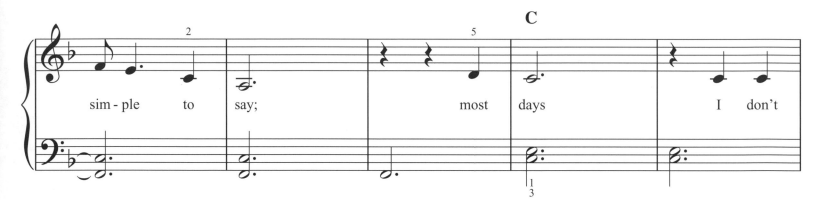

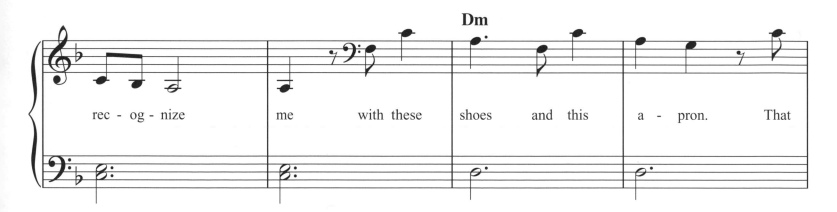

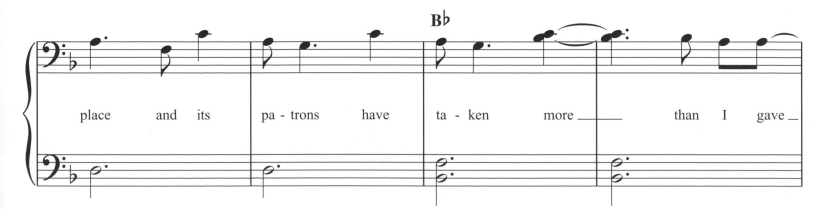

_____ them. It's not eas - y to know; _____

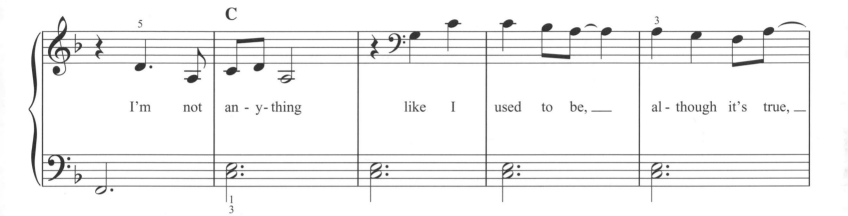

**C**

I'm not an - y-thing like I used to be, ___ al - though it's true, ___

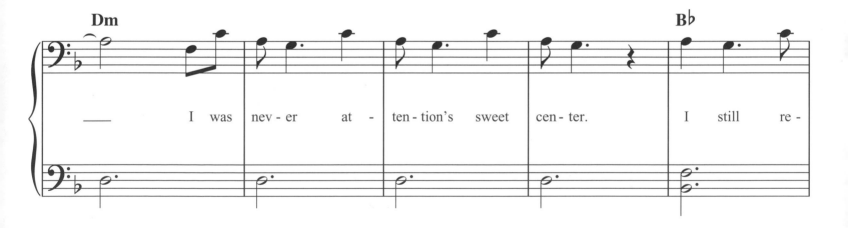

**Dm** **B♭**

_____ I was nev - er at - ten - tion's sweet cen - ter. I still re -

**F**

mem - ber that ___ girl: She's im - per - fect, _____ but she

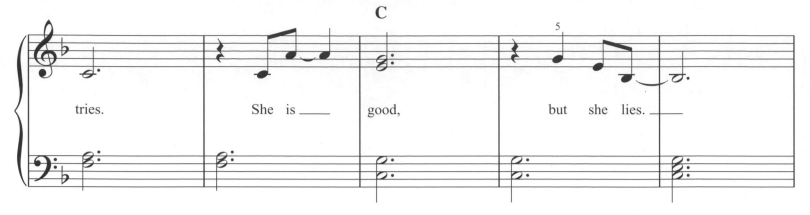

tries.　　　　She is ___ good,　　　but she lies. ___

She is ___ hard _____ on her - self. ___　　　She is

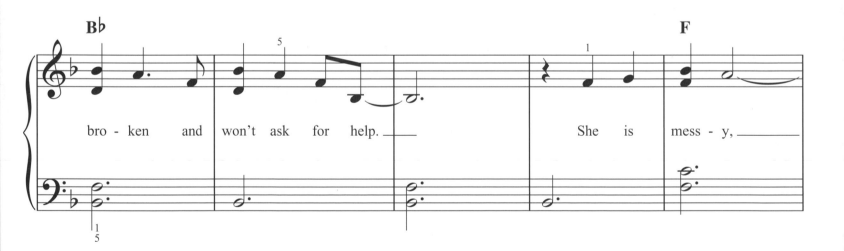

bro - ken　and won't ask for help. ___　　　She is mess - y, ___

___ but she's kind.　　　She is ___ lone - ly ___

most of the time.____ She is all of this,____ mixed up and

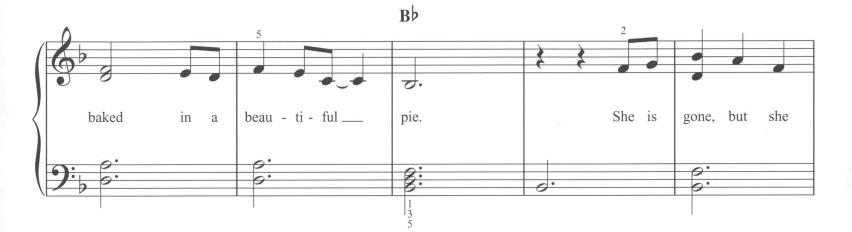

baked in a beau - ti - ful____ pie. She is gone, but she

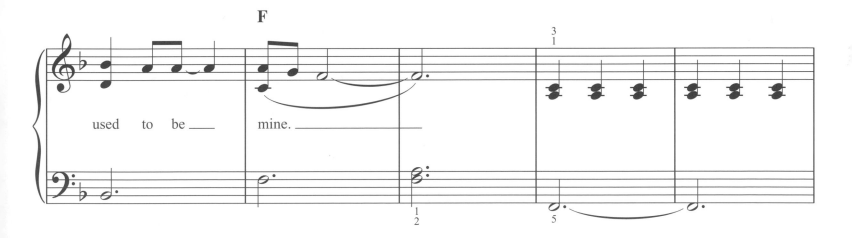

used to be ____ mine. _____

It's not ____ what I asked for. Some - times life _____

just slips in through a back door and carves out a

per - son and makes you be - lieve it's all true, and

now I've got you. And you're not what I asked for.

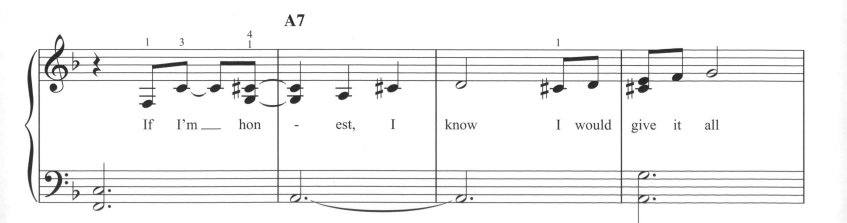

If I'm hon - est, I know I would give it all

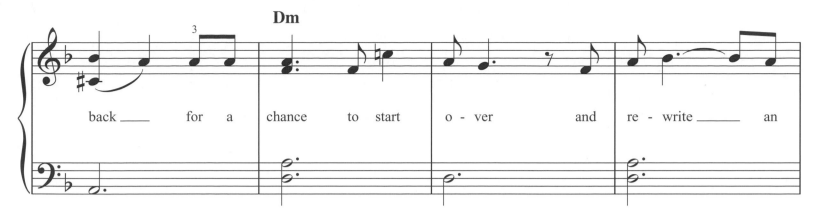

and gets used ___ by a man who can't ___ love. ___ And

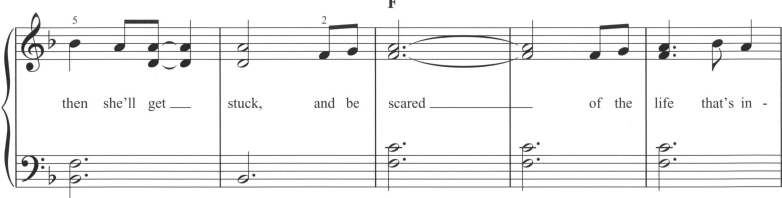

then she'll get ___ stuck, and be scared ___ of the life that's in -

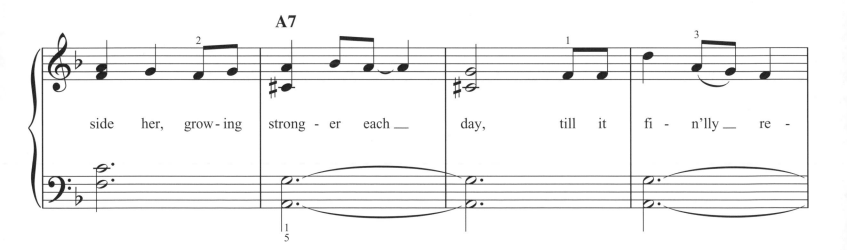

side her, grow-ing strong - er each ___ day, till it fi - n'lly ___ re -

minds her to fight just a lit - tle to bring back the fire ___

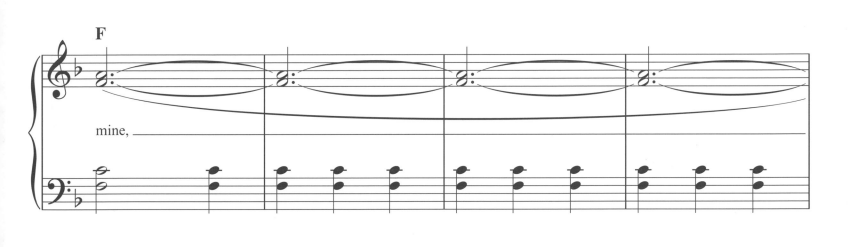

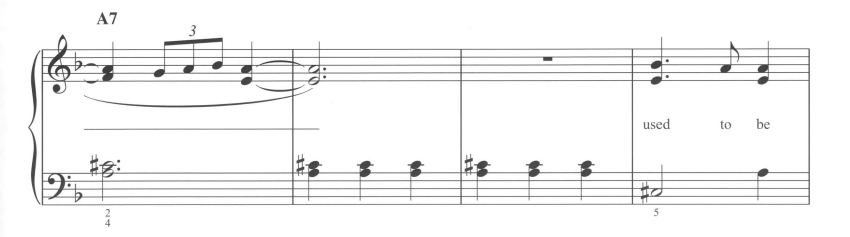

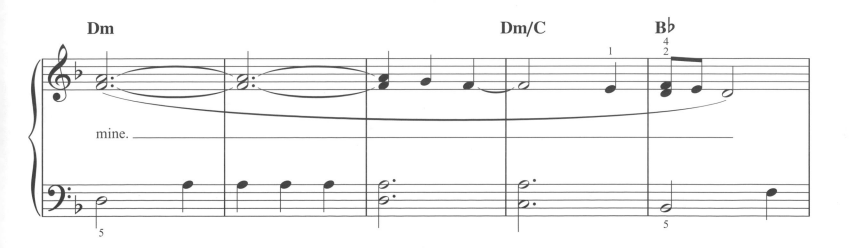

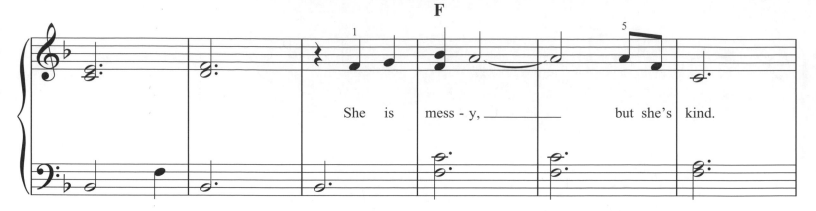

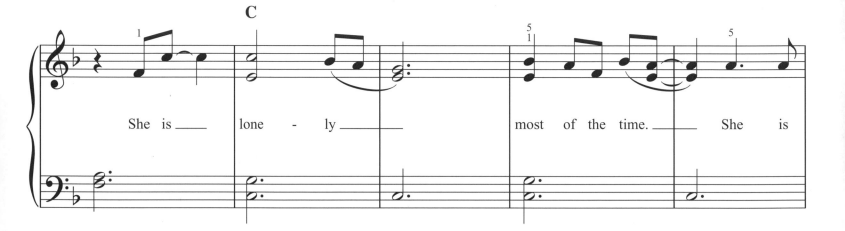

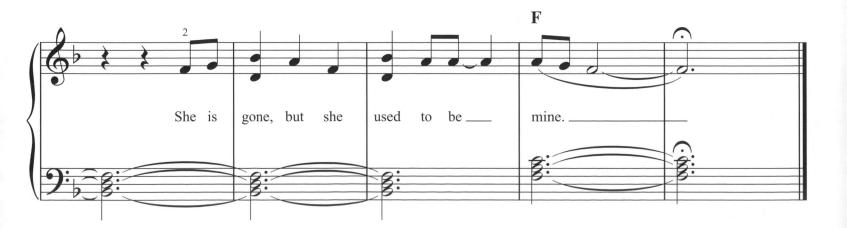

# THIS TOWN

Words and Music by NIALL HORAN,
MICHAEL NEEDLE, DANIEL BRYER
and JAMIE SCOTT

**Moderate Folk feel**

Wak-ing up ___ to kiss you, and

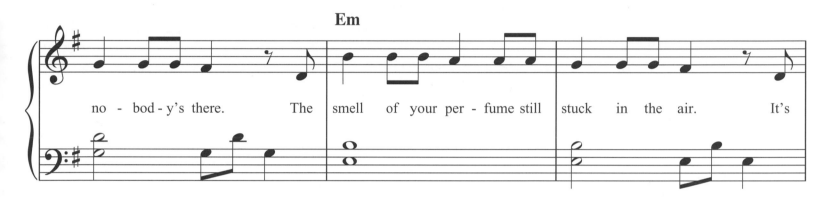

no-bod-y's there. The smell of your per-fume still stuck in the air. It's

hard. _____

Yes-ter-day, ___ I thought I saw your
saw ___ that you moved ___ on with

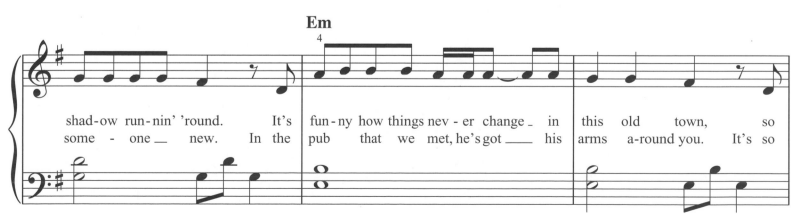

shad-ow run-nin' 'round. It's fun-ny how things nev-er change ___ in this old town, so
some-one ___ new. In the pub that we met, he's got ___ his arms a-round you. It's so

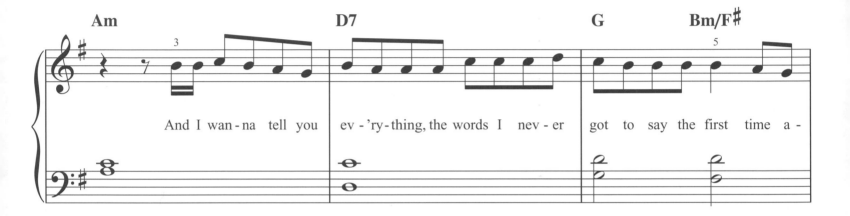

If the whole world was watch - ing, I'd still dance with you; drive

high - ways and by - ways to be there with you. O - ver and o - ver, the

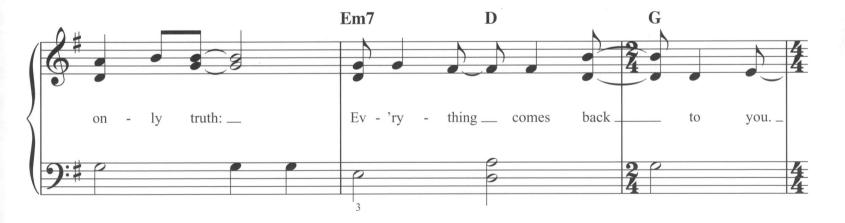

on - ly truth: ___ Ev - 'ry - thing ___ comes back ___ to you. ___

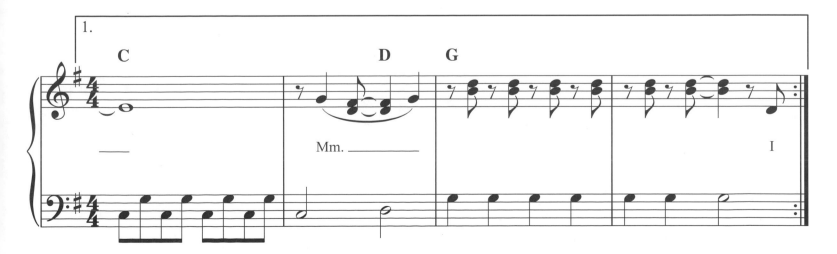

___ Mm. ___ I

You still make me ner-vous when you walk in the room. Them

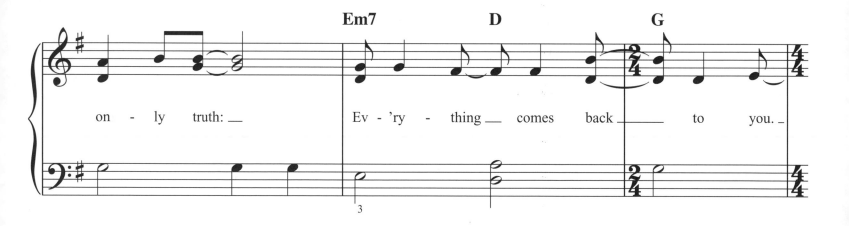

but-ter-flies, __ they come a-live __ when I'm next to you. O - ver and o - ver, the

on - ly truth: __ Ev - 'ry - thing __ comes back __ to you. __

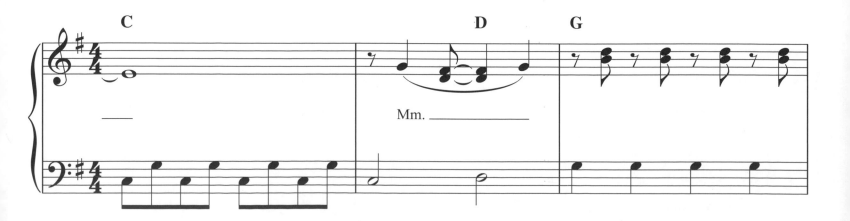

Mm. __

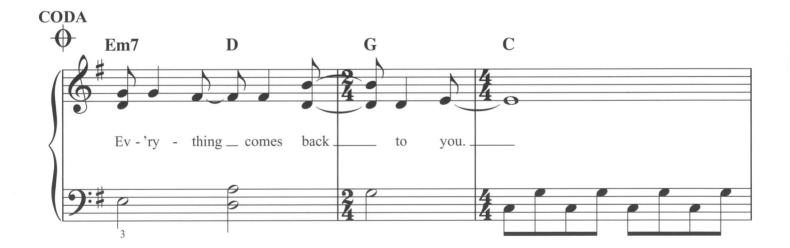

# STAND BY YOU

Words and Music by RACHEL PLATTEN,
JOY WILLIAMS, JACK ANTONOFF,
JON LEVINE and MATTHEW B. MORRIS

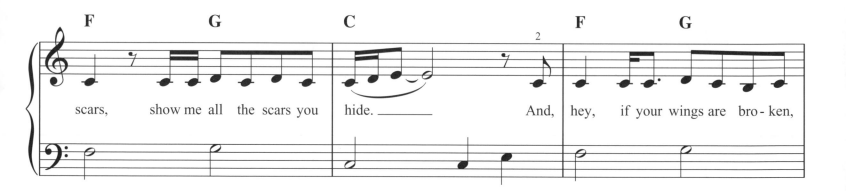

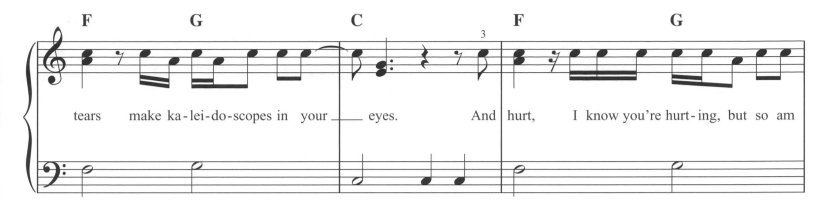

tears make ka-lei-do-scopes in your ___ eyes. And hurt, I know you're hurt-ing, but so am

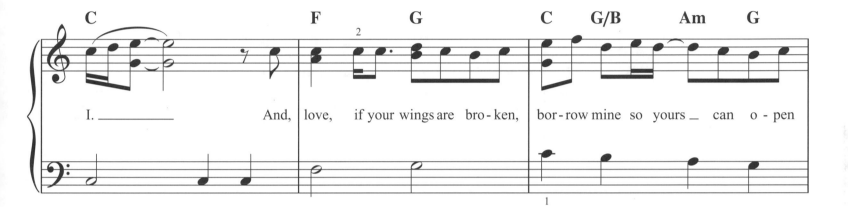

I. ___ And, love, if your wings are bro-ken, bor-row mine so yours ___ can o-pen

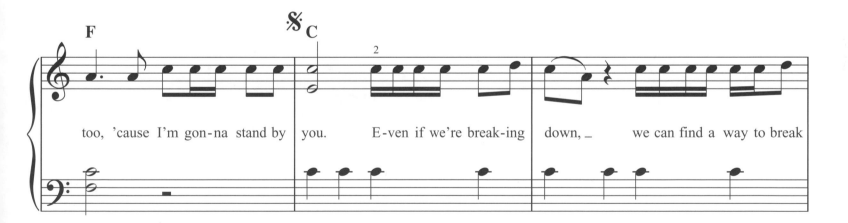

too, 'cause I'm gon-na stand by you. E-ven if we're break-ing down, ___ we can find a way to break

through. ___ E-ven if we can't find heav-en, I'll walk through hell with you. ___ Love, ___ you're not a-lone, ___

'cause I'm gon-na stand by you. E-ven if we can't find heav-en, I'm gon-na stand by

you. _ E-ven if we can't find heav-en, I'll walk through hell with you. _ Love, _ you're not a-lone, _

**To Coda** ⊕

'cause I'm gon-na stand by you. Yeah, you're all I nev-er knew I need-ed. And the

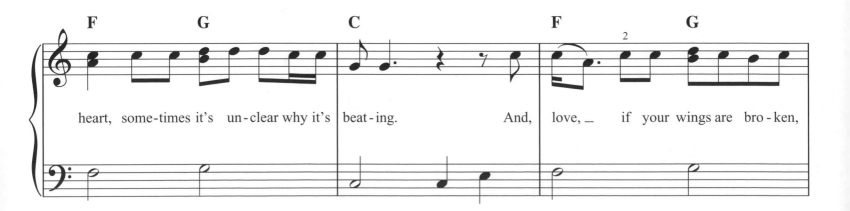

heart, some-times it's un-clear why it's beat-ing. And, love, _ if your wings are bro-ken,

we can brave through those _ e-mo-tions too, 'cause I'm gon-na stand by you. And, oh, ____

truth, I guess truth is what you be-lieve in. ____ And faith, I think faith is hav-ing a

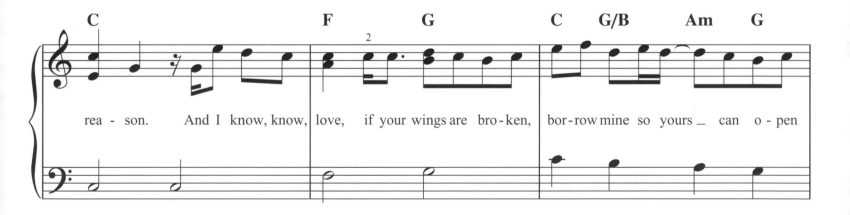

rea-son. And I know, know, love, if your wings are bro-ken, bor-row mine so yours _ can o-pen

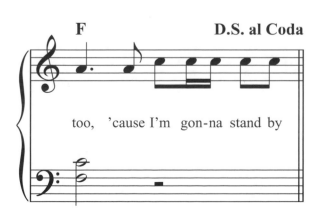

too, 'cause I'm gon-na stand by

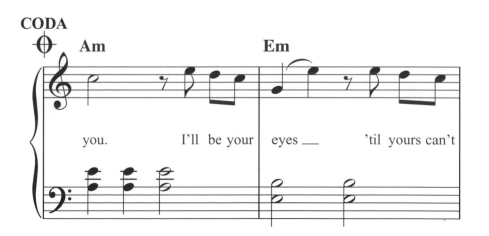

you. I'll be your eyes ___ 'til yours can't

shine.        And I'll  be your  arms, I'll be ____ your stead - y  sat - el - lite. ____        And when you can't

rise,        well, I'll  crawl with you  on hands and  knees, 'cause  I, _____ I'm gon-na  stand by

you.        E -ven if we're break-ing  down, _        we can find a  way to break  through. _        E -ven if we can't find

heav- en,        I'll walk through hell with you. ____        Love, _ you're not  a -lone, ____        'cause I'm gon-na  stand by

# UNSTEADY

Words and Music by ALEXANDER JUNIOR GRANT,
ADAM LEVIN, CASEY HARRIS,
NOAH FELDSHUH and SAM HARRIS

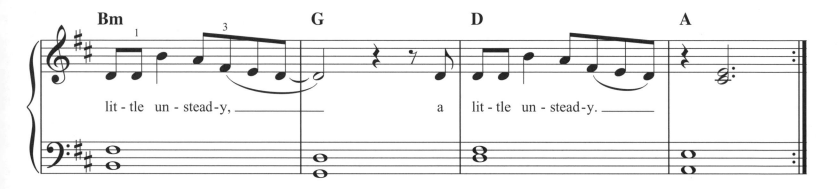

Hold, _____ hold _____ on, _____ hold on to me. 'Cause I'm a

lit - tle un - stead - y, _____ a lit - tle un - stead - y. _____

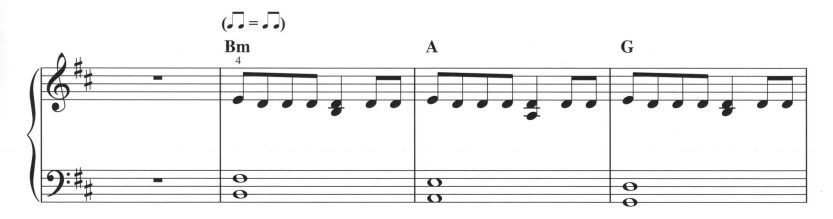

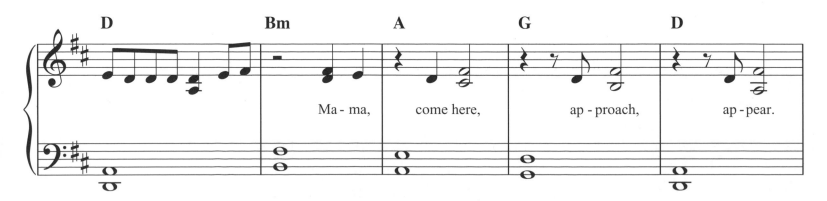

Ma - ma, come here, ap - proach, ap - pear.

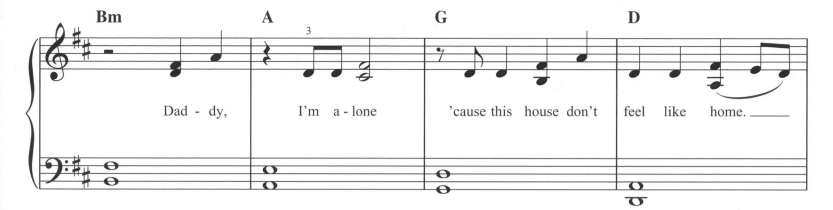

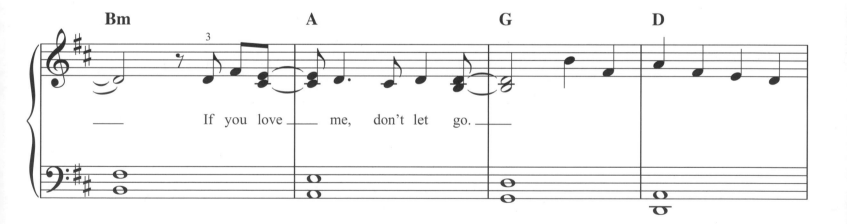

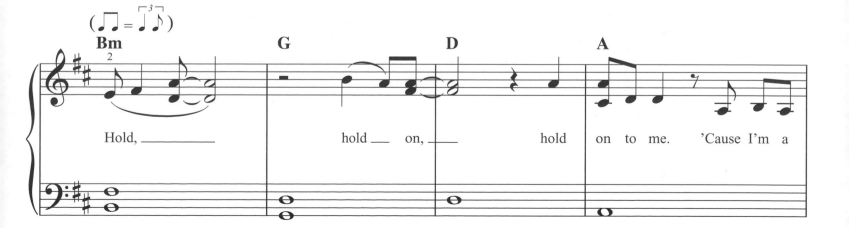

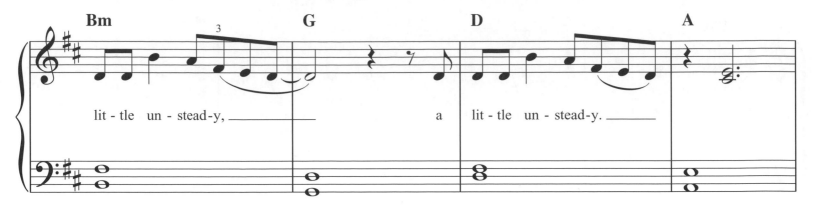

**Bm** | **G** | **D** | **A**

lit - tle un - stead-y, _____ a lit - tle un - stead-y. _____

**Bm** | **G** | **D** | **A**

Hold, _____ hold ___ on, _____ hold on to me. 'Cause I'm a

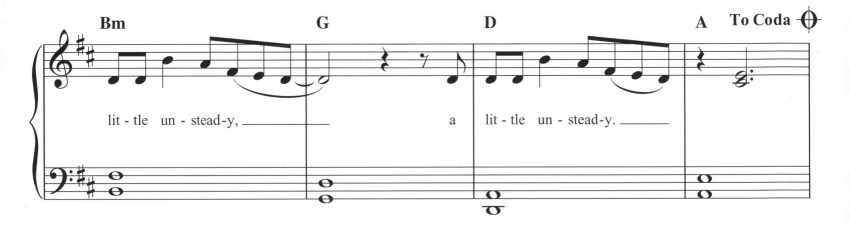

**Bm** | **G** | **D** | **A** **To Coda**

lit - tle un - stead-y, _____ a lit - tle un - stead-y. _____

**Bm** | **A** | **G** | **D**

Moth - er, I know that you're tired of be - ing a - lone.

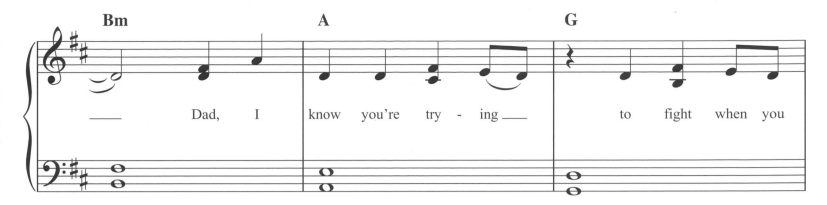

Dad, I know you're try - ing ___ to fight when you

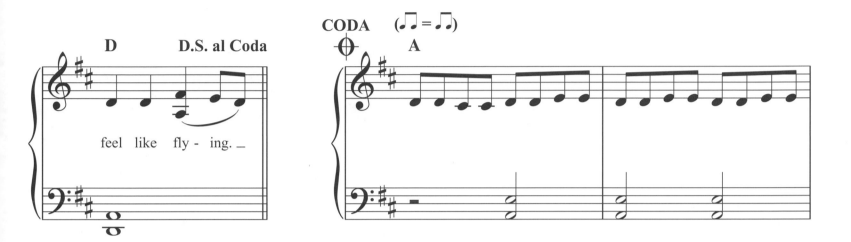

feel like fly - ing. __

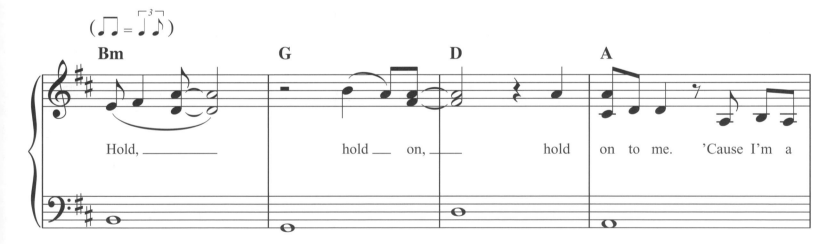

Hold, _____ hold __ on, ___ hold on to me. 'Cause I'm a

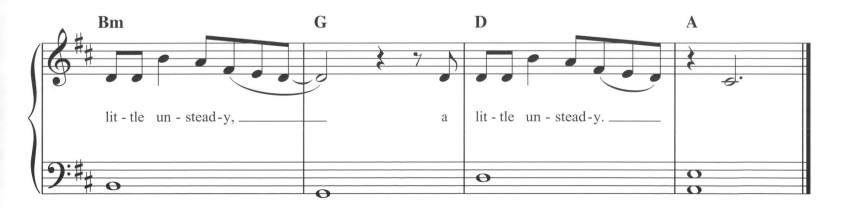

lit - tle un - stead - y, ___ a lit - tle un - stead - y. ___

# VERSACE ON THE FLOOR

Words and Music by BRUNO MARS,
PHILIP LAWRENCE, JAMES FAUNTLEROY
and CHRISTOPHER BRODY BROWN

Moderately slow

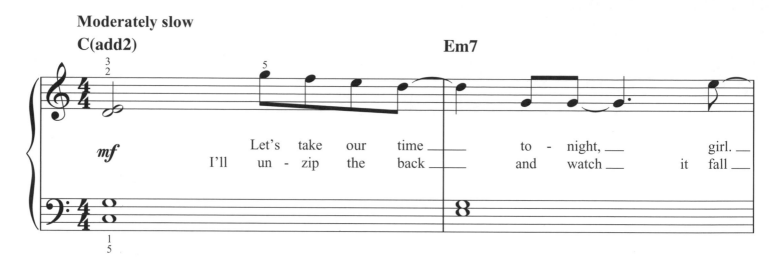

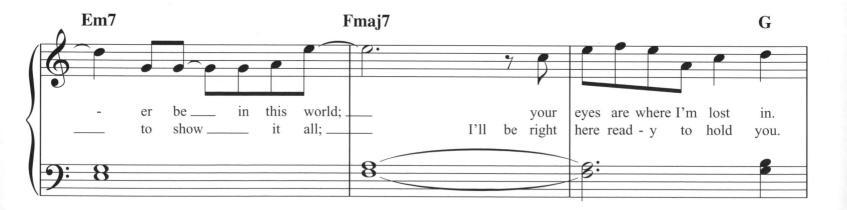

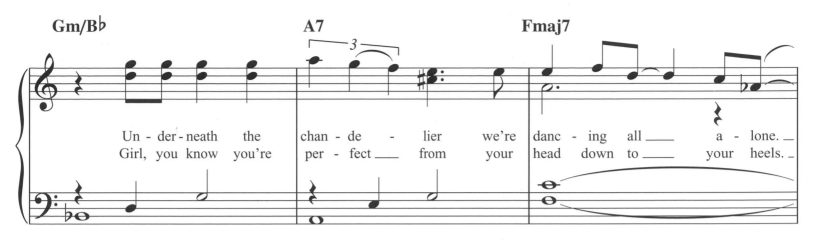

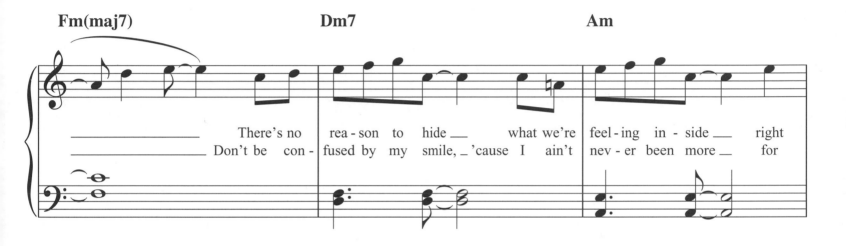

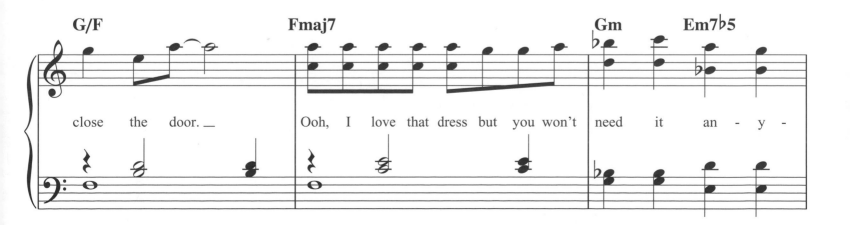

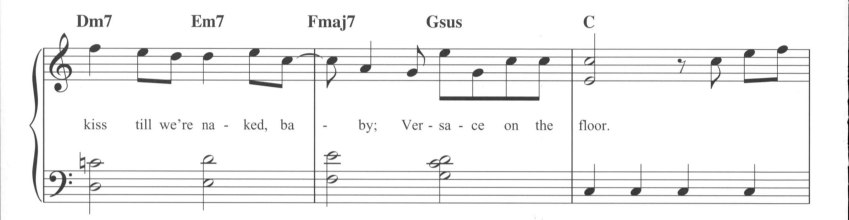

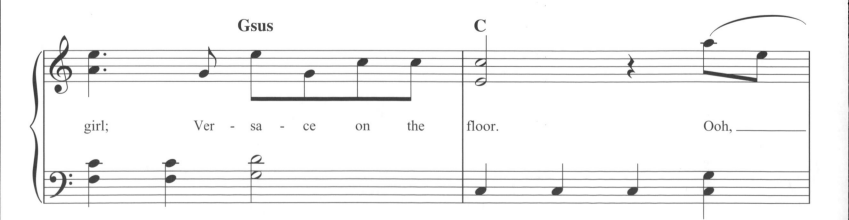

take it off for me, \_\_\_ for me, \_\_\_ for me, \_\_\_ for me, \_\_\_ now

**To Coda**

**1.** **Gsus**

girl.

**2.** **Gsus** **D.S. al Coda**

girl.

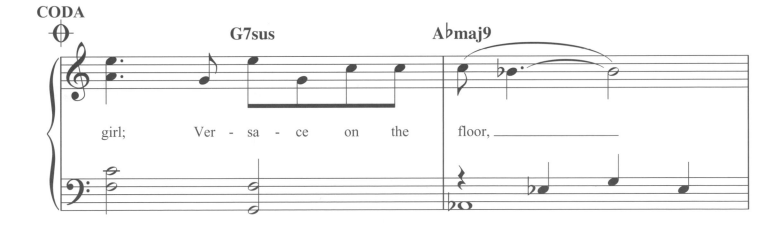

**CODA**

**G7sus** **A♭maj9**

girl; Ver - sa - ce on the floor, \_\_\_

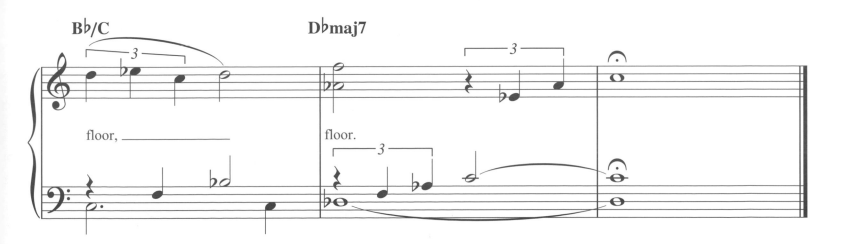

**B♭/C** **D♭maj7**

floor, \_\_\_ floor.

# WHEN WE WERE YOUNG

Words and Music by ADELE ADKINS
and TOBIAS JESSO JR.

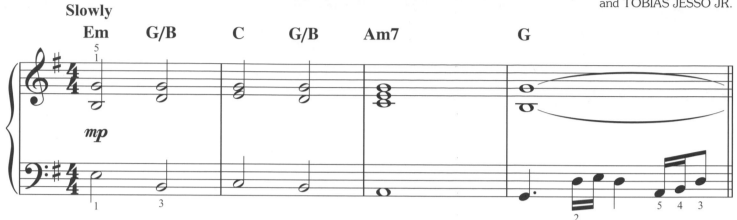

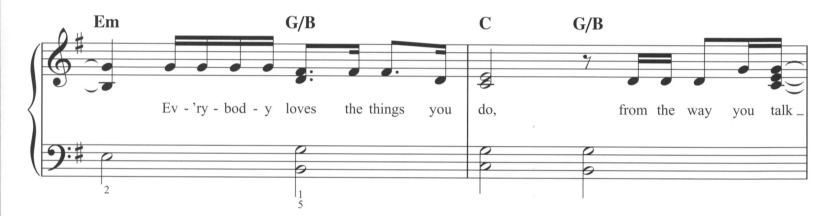

Ev-'ry-bod-y loves the things you do, from the way you talk

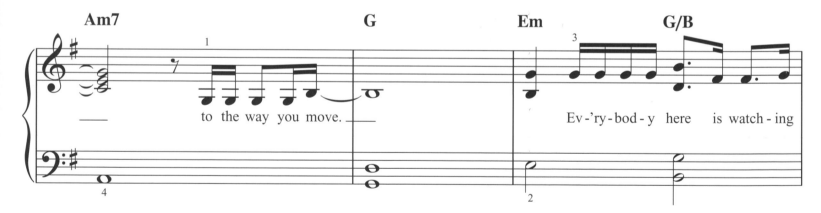

to the way you move. Ev-'ry-bod-y here is watch-ing

you, 'cause you feel like home, you're like a dream come true.

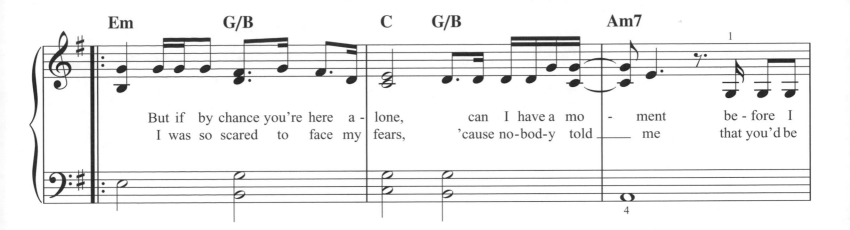

But if by chance you're here a - lone,   can I have a mo - ment   be - fore I
I was so scared to face my fears,   'cause no-bod-y told ___ me   that you'd be

go? _____   'Cause I've been by   my - self all night  long,   hop - ing you're
here. _____   And   I swear you'd moved o - ver -  seas:   that's what you

some - one ___   I used to  know.   You   look like a mov - ie,   you sound like a
said _____   when you left  me.   You still look like a mov - ie,   you still sound like a

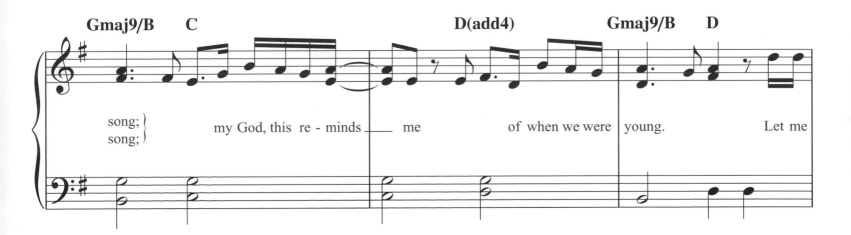

song;   my God, this re - minds ___ me   of when we were  young.   Let me
song;

pho - to - graph __ you in this light, in case __ it is the last __ time that we

might be ex - act - ly like we were be - fore we re - al - ized we were

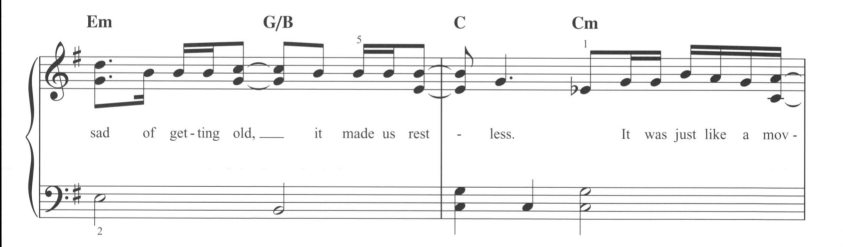

sad of get - ting old, __ it made us rest - less. It was just like a mov -

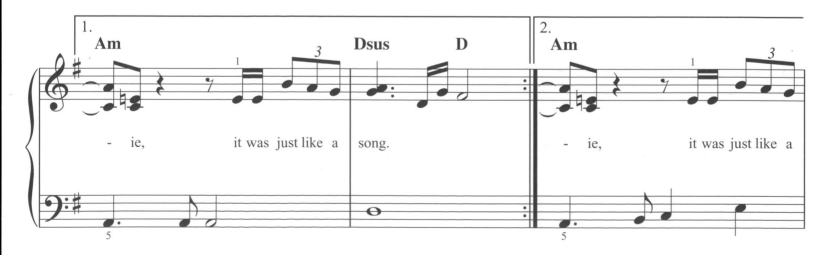

1.
- ie, it was just like a song.

2.
- ie, it was just like a

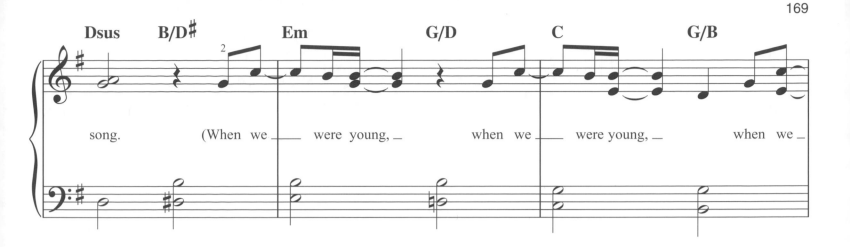

song. (When we ___ were young, ___ when we ___ were young, ___ when we ___

___ were young, ___ when we ___ were young.) ___ It's hard to win ___ me there.

Ev - 'ry - thing just takes me back ___ to when you were there, ___ to when

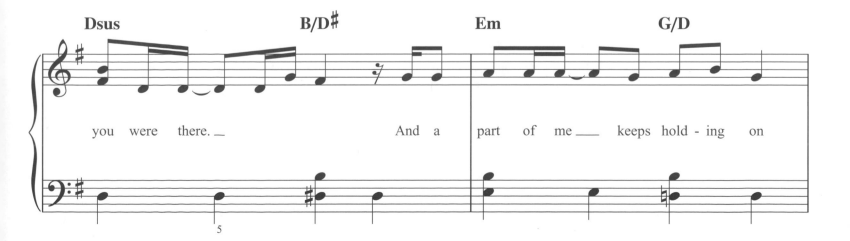

you were there. ___ And a part of me ___ keeps hold - ing on

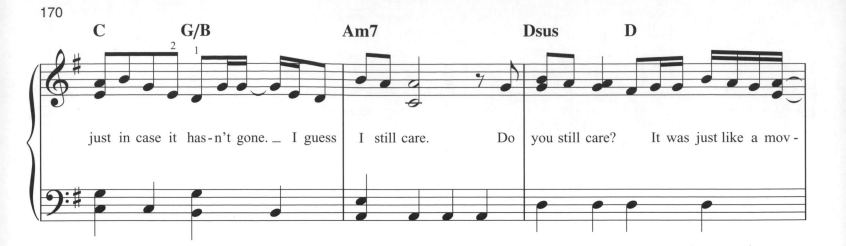

just in case it has-n't gone. _ I guess I still care. Do you still care? It was just like a mov-

- ie, it was just like a song. My God, this re - minds _ me of when we were

young. _____ (When we were young, _ when we _ were young, _ when we _

_ were young, _ when we _ were young.) _ Let me pho-to-graph _ you in this light, in case _

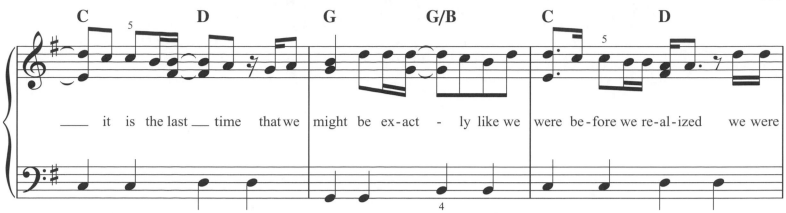

_____ it is the last _____ time that we might be ex-act - ly like we were be-fore we re-al-ized we were

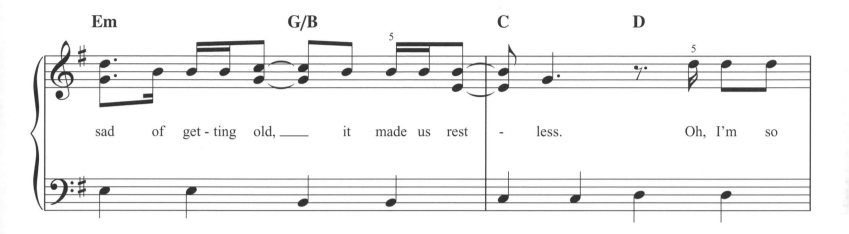

sad of get-ting old, _____ it made us rest - less. Oh, I'm so

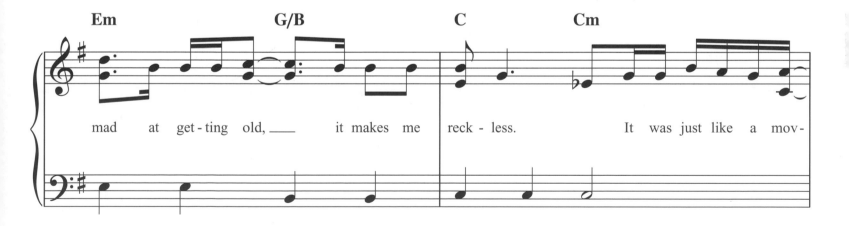

mad at get-ting old, _____ it makes me reck - less. It was just like a mov-

- ie, it was just like a song _____ when we were young.

# WRITING'S ON THE WALL

from the film SPECTRE

Words and Music by SAM SMITH
and JAMES NAPIER

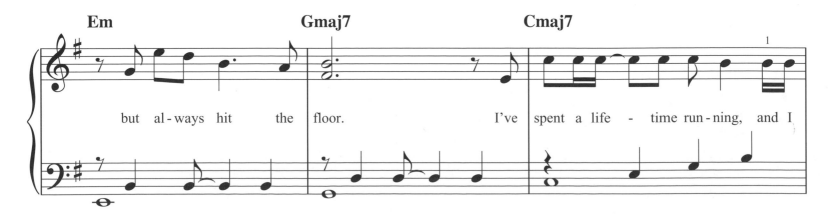

al-ways get a-way. __ But with you, I'm feel-ing some - thing that makes me want to stay. __

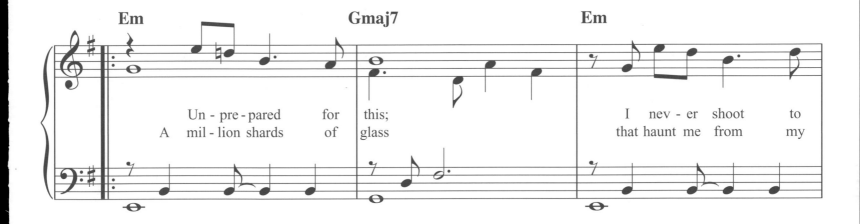

Un - pre-pared for this;
A mil - lion shards of glass

I nev - er shoot to
that haunt me from my

miss.
past.

But I feel like a storm is com - ing if I'm
As the stars be - gin to gath - er, and the

gon - na make it through the day. __ And there's no more use in run - ning, this is
light __ be - gins to fade, __ when all hope be - gins to shat - ter, know that

some-thing I've got - ta face. __
I _____ will be a - fraid. __

If I risk it all, _____

could you break our fall?

How could I

live? How do I breathe? When you're not here, I'm suf - fo - cat - ing. I wan - na feel

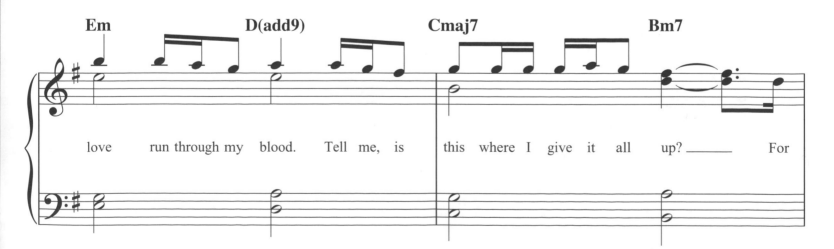

love run through my blood. Tell me, is this where I give it all up? _____ For

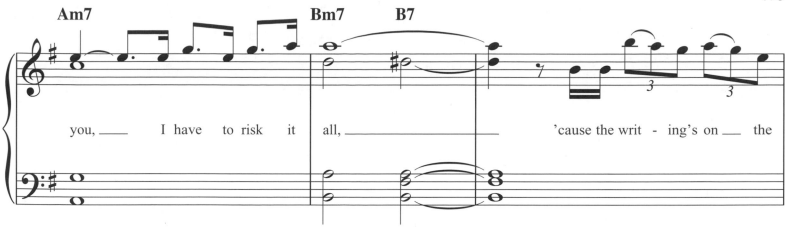

you, ___ I have to risk it all, _____ 'cause the writ - ing's on ___ the

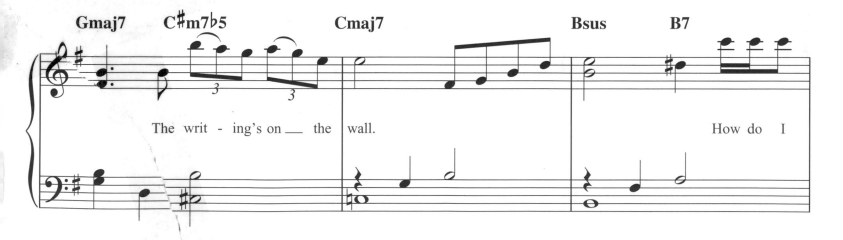

1.
wall.

2.
wall.

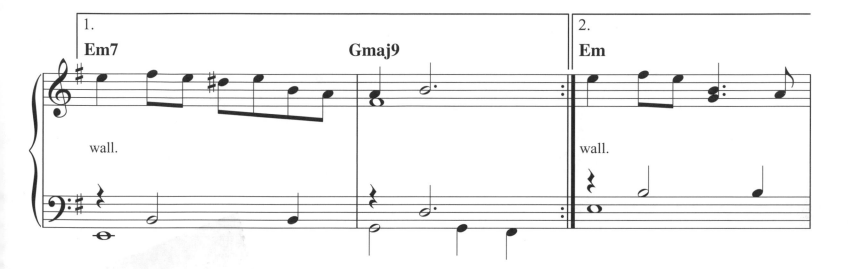

The writ - ing's on ___ the wall. How do I

live? How do I breathe? When you're not here, I'm suf - fo - cat - ing. I wan - na feel